The Populace
in Shakespeare

Brents Stirling

NEW YORK: COLUMBIA UNIVERSITY PRESS

1949

.ٍ

Published in Great Britain, Canada
and India by Geoffrey Cumberlege
Oxford University Press
London, Toronto, and Bombay

To A. W. S.

Acknowledgments

DURING THE SUMMER of 1942 a fellowship granted by the Henry E. Huntington Library made possible the collection of material found in the fourth chapter of this book. Accordingly, I wish to express my deepest gratitude to the trustees of the library and its staff and to acknowledge also the publication in digest form of some of my findings by the *Huntington Library Quarterly*.

To my colleagues in the English Department of the University of Washington, particularly to Professor Allen R. Benham and the late Professors Ray Heffner and Frederick M. Padelford, I owe much for helpful suggestion. Messrs. Godfrey Davies, of the Huntington Library, and Louis Wright, now of the Folger Library, contributed valuable criticism at an early stage of writing. It is understood, of course, that my interpretations do not necessarily coincide with the points of view of those who have helped me. I also wish to acknowledge the indispensable assistance of my wife, both in preparation of materials and in checking proofs.

Publication of this book has been facilitated in part by a generous grant from the Agnes H. Anderson Research Fund of the University of Washington. I am very grateful for this assistance.

BRENTS STIRLING

Seattle, Wash.
January 3, 1949

Contents

The Populace in Shakespeare

CHAPTER I

Literature and Society: Some Current Problems

THE OCCASIONAL ventilation of scholarship in order to discover just where, if anywhere, we are going is one of the obligations a scholar owes to the community which maintains him, and it should be one of his more congenial activities. Congenial or not, it is seldom easy, because "first principles" are infrequently stated; a critic's fundamental position generally is to be found among his tacit reservations and his unconscious biases. One's primary obligation is to analyze these factors and, if possible, to formulate them in preliminary discussion.

Two problems are to be encountered in this chapter. The first is raised by current attacks upon the historical interpretation of literature, particularly that in which literature is questioned as a causative agent in social evolution. The second problem is to state a few restraints and obligations which those engaged in social studies of literature may find it profitable to recognize.

If a critic writes about character motivation in Shakespeare, few will charge him with trying to exhibit Shakespeare primarily as a psychologist and secondarily as an artist. Should he choose, however, to approach the many-sided dramatist from a political point of view, he is likely to be asked whether he thinks of Shakespeare as a pamphleteer. To this depressing question there is, of course, the answer that good playwriting always transcends pamphleteering. But rejoinder to this answer may suggest that politics is at best a banal subject and that one should be ashamed of one's self. With a little heat, reply is now made that politics is concerned with human groups in conflict or in equilibrium, and as such can only be banal when dealt with in banal fashion. At this point in an unhappy argument the opposition may shift ground by declaring that social and political interpretation of literature is old-fashioned; that sophisticated people are turning to the writing of truly literary history in place of that in which literature as an art appears "merely as a troublesome wrapper for the ideas studied." [1] And of this asocial preoccupation with the growth of literary forms, Louis Wright has remarked that it would resemble a history of hat design which stresses the evolution of hat geometry from Euclid onward, and pays no attention to people who wore the hats.[2]

Plainly, there are those who favor the social-historical approach to literature and those who do not, and one is often tempted thus to close the issue. To do so here, however, would be both a simplification and an evasion, for the actual course of this controversy at an intelligent level has involved well-justified attacks by each side upon the other. The traditional historical critics reacted adversely against whim, intuition, and anachronism on the part of those who wrote of Shakespeare as though he were an Elizabethan Byron, a nineteenth-century novelist, or a present-day social humanitarian. But the traditional historical school then presented us, fact by fact, with the "Elizabethan Shakespeare," whose characters are explained by a specialized and now outmoded psychology (Elizabethans explained character mainly in that way), whose plays contain little personal conviction (standardized beliefs are never projected with personal fervor), whose social views were conventionally Elizabethan (all Elizabethan dramatists

---

[1] René Welleck, "The Nature and Scope of Literary History," *Huntington Library Quarterly,* VI (Nov., 1942), 35–39. Paper read at the Huntington Library Research Conference, 1942.

[2] Observations upon Mr. Welleck's paper, *ibid.,* p. 43.

held Elizabethan social views). And so forth. Any individual representative of the historical school recognizes that this amorphous being is not Shakespeare, that not all Elizabethans thought alike, and that even had they done so, the hold of Shakespeare upon us persists, not because of, but in spite of his identification with much of the Elizabethan norm. Unfortunately, however, no representative of the historical school can do much to clarify the collective impression it has made. This, when pardonably oversimplified by students and others, is that if we understand Elizabethan society and Elizabethan attitudes we understand Shakespeare. The historical interpreter, of course, will disavow such a notion; all he means is that we cannot grasp Shakespeare unless we first understand the Elizabethan milieu, and that critical evaluation does not end with such understanding but begins with it. It is well known, however, that historical critics have not generally tried to evaluate or to explain literary artistry, and more often than not have rested after fragmentary presentation of historical fact. This fault of practice rather than of theory has led Mr. Wellek and others to observe that we have persistently left the writing of truly literary history to succeeding generations.[3] The critics he represents would stress, as a corrective measure, the evolution of literary values and forms instead of what they consider to be a swirl of historical data which remains irrelevant as long as the evolution of art is not made paramount.

One of the dullest positions into which a critic can maneuver himself is that of mediating between opposites. The truth about a subject is usually a by-product of the clash between extremists who feel and think strongly enough to project their necks from their collars; evolution of knowledge, of social institutions, and of artistic forms proceeds largely in this fashion, and the judicial temperament is often complimented for ability to synthesize what has already been

[3] *Ibid.*, p. 36.

discerned by most sensible people interested in the subject. Accordingly, it is hoped that nothing written here will be interpreted as an attempt to show enthusiasts their errors or to derive placid truth from the excessive claims of antagonists. If a scholar believes that the evolution of Shakespeare's verse in its adaptation to dramatic dialogue is a fundamental problem, while the political background of Elizabethan mob scenes is sociological and extraneous to literature, he probably means that he is interested in the first question and rather bored by the second. But he should not hesitate to put this bias into print, for it is only by frank expression that specialized attitudes can be prevented from assuming orthodoxy and "objectivity," or from standardizing seminars the country over. Probably what both the historical school and the historical-esthetic school fear most is that the opposed view will become thus dominant. To agree that neither should become dominant, however, is not to agree that either should be silent.

One very forthright position which social-historical critics can assert is that humanistic study in a world of crisis should be concerned with social factors simply because our crisis is a social one. And if objection is entered that this negates values of artistry, reply can be made that it does so no more than the study of history inhibits the study of poetry. The more subtle dissenters, however, attempt a different attack: the study of literature and society, they say, has no materiality, for it is plain that while art may reflect social evolution it does not influence it.

> For poetry makes nothing happen: it survives
> In the valley of its saying where executives
> Would never want to tamper; it flows south
> From ranches of isolation and the busy griefs,
> Raw towns that we believe and die in; it survives,
> A way of happening, a mouth.[4]

[4] "In Memory of W. B. Yeats," in *The Collected Poetry of W. H. Auden* (New York, Random House, 1945), pp. 48–51. Reprinted by permission of Random House, Inc.

Should Mr. Auden's lines be construed merely as loose and suggestive, there is another and a much more pointed statement of the case by one of his characters, the defense counsel in *The Public vs. the Late William Butler Yeats.*

For art is a product of history, not a cause. Unlike some other products, technical inventions for example, it does not re-enter history as an effective agent, so that the question whether art should or should not be propaganda is unreal. The case for the prosecution rests on the fallacious belief that art ever makes anything happen, whereas the honest truth, gentlemen, is that, if not a poem had been written, not a picture painted, not a bar of music composed, the history of man would be materially unchanged.[5]

It would seem that Shelley's "unacknowledged legislators" are lame-duck congressmen.

Most of us have from time to time entertained similiar beliefs; Mr. Auden is the persuasive spokesman of a rather common notion. And it should be recalled that almost all traditional consideration of the relationship between literature and society has dealt with the influence of social movements upon literature, not with that of literature upon social movements. It is ironical, for example, that Max Lerner's book *Ideas Are Weapons* should contain a major chapter on literature and society in which literature, far from being considered as a weapon, is discussed as a product of social forces.[6]

If it is true that literature in relation to social evolution is symptomatic rather than causal, scholarship and criticism are, of course, in the same category, and no moral obligation should tempt a practical man to deal with the social side of these pursuits. The only sound motive he could have for doing so is that activity of this sort interests him, and the whole issue might therefore be written off as subjective. For if the premise of Mr. Auden's defense counsel is assumed, even a

[5] *Partisan Review,* Spring, 1939. Reprinted by permission of *The Partisan Review.*

[6] Mr. Lerner does not confine his discussion elsewhere in the book to this one-way process.

modest clarification of the processes of social change by literary men is not the kind of clarification which assists or retards the social movements involved. The author or critic either helps to illuminate issues and events *ex post facto,* or his illumination is not influential enough or cogent enough to have more than esthetic or descriptive results.

Dogma as congenial and as economical as Mr. Auden's should never be met humorlessly or consecutively. But it must be met, nevertheless. Perhaps issue may be joined adequately if a few questions are asked of this agreeable heresy. There need be no staying for answers except on the part of readers who have the commendable habit of thinking for themselves and who know that simple problems require thoughtful solutions.

If we are asked to believe that literature and literary criticism are but symptomatic ripples in the social tide, we may inquire first whether this means merely that they are indirect causes of social change: whether the ultimate issue of their existence as causes is confused with the undeniable difficulty of isolating them as such. Other potential meanings press hard on the heels of this one. Does the noncausal view of poetry, drama, and other fiction merely imply that these arts often do exist merely as social symptoms? Does it mean that they can be accepted as conservers of the *status quo,* but not as instruments of social change? Does it signify merely that the primary purpose of art is to edify rather than to educate? At the risk of dogmatism it may be observed that all these possible meanings are irrelevant to the main issue.

Mr. Auden's defense counsel, however, is far from unaware of this main problem when he asserts that "if not a poem had been written . . . the history of man would be materially unchanged." But even this frontal declaration is an unconscious evasion, because it is scarcely poetry as a separate factor which affects history; it is rather poetry as part of a complex of forces. History does not contain simple and isolable ingredients. If we inquire, not about poetry in isolation, but about group thought and feeling, of which poems are an important expression, some very different issues materialize. Has the noble-savage cult been uninfluential? Social behavior is still influenced by lingering idealization of man in uncomplicated surroundings. Is the golden-age myth unperpetuated and ineffective? A. N. Whitehead has suggested that "nothing does more harm in unnerving men for their duties in the present than the attention devoted to points of excellence in the past as compared with the average failure of the present day." [7] Or has the heritage of Byron been inoperative in various "lost generation" philosophies of defeat and inaction during the last quarter century? Has the romantic love tradition, with its heritage of top-heavy idealism in courtship, been unrelated to the divorce rate? On the credit side, the noble savage and the golden-age traditions have served as contrasts against which political oppression, materialism, and uncontrolled industrialism have been made to stand out in a peculiarly effective manner. Byronism has been valuable in facilitating adverse reaction to false idealism and narrow convention. And the rapture of Romeo has not been unconnected with disappearance of parentally arranged marriages. These observations suggest still another illustration: what of the school of sensibility? While it is true that the bleeding-heart cult has taken dubious form among antivivisectionists and sentimental ameliorists of poverty, who will say that kindlier treatment of animals, of the poor, of the insane, and of children has not advanced with its impetus?

These illustrations, however, may not meet squarely the skeptic's argument. It is true, he may say, that such changes for good and bad have occurred and that poetry, novels, plays, and criticism were of some influence in causing them to

[7] *Science and the Modern World* (New York, The Macmillan Company, 1928), p. 294.

occur. But, he continues, they would have occurred in any event, or even had the force of literature been arrayed against rather than for their occurrence. This hypothetical state of affairs is truly a poser. We are asked to imagine what history would have been if some of the history had been left out. We are asked, moreover, to entertain a conception of social evolution from which there has been removed not only the chief outlet for imagination and feeling but the one art form in which there is extensive communication of ideas. Would English nationalism have flourished in the sixteenth century, for example, had there been no Shakespeare, Spenser, Daniel, Warner, or minor poets and dramatists of patriotism, not to mention authors of ballads and unrecorded lore which happened to cross the borderline into poetry? The only possible reply is that one lacks the remotest idea whether English nationalism would have flourished under these conditions, and after such an answer one may say to the skeptic in parting: "This was your idea; if you wish to determine what social evolution would have been without literature, you may set up the controls and run the experiment." To demonstrate the intuition that poetry makes nothing happen requires a kind of historical laboratory which historians scarcely possess.

If it is agreed that literature and historical scholarship may have contributed to social evolution, historians who feel a moral obligation to develop this relationship are justified in continuing the emphasis. There is, however, enough indirection in the connection between literature and social movements to discourage apostledom or torch-bearing. Certainly, if it is to be anything, the social-historical aspect of literary effort and interpretation should be modest; the writer, the critic, and least of all the scholar can scarcely claim the distinction of being an acknowledged or even unacknowledged legislator. Humility, however, can be practiced as a virtue without the embracing of timidity or ineffectuality.

In the social interpretation of literature there are a number of specific practices which can be avoided, as well as some obligations which should be assumed. Among the former is impulsiveness or naïveté in shaping authors of the past into spokesmen for what may be the present social views of the critic or scholar. There have been several efforts, which can only be called depressing, to place Shakespeare and other writers of the past in the vanguard of modern liberalism, either by quoting them out of context or by assuming uncritically that they anticipated modern developments. This is not to say that all such interpretation has been uncritical. In the case of Shakespeare, moreover, it can be suggested that an equally questionable practice is to make him speak for modern conservatism, on the assumption that his Elizabethan feeling for social hierarchy can be applied to modern conditions. If it appears that the Elizabethan populace suffers at Shakespeare's hands, it should be enough for the social critic to demonstrate that there was an issue of democracy during Elizabethan times, to state it in Elizabethan terms, and to show its significance in history.

Another shortcoming which such an interpretation may avoid is neglect of literary values. This does not mean that emphasis must be placed upon appraisal of style and technique or that social issues should be discussed only as they seem to influence literary forms. Nor does it mean that one should not on occasion be interested in third-rate writers when they happen to be influential. In the field of Shakespeare it means simply that an interpreter of social themes should try to communicate the quality as well as the nature of Shakespeare's contribution and that a historian of Elizabethan social attitudes should not be insensitive to emotional or formal elements shown by Elizabethan writers. All this is easy to formulate as a body of principle; the difficulty arises in attempting to implement it. There is perhaps but one way of doing this: [8] that of allowing authors who supply material to speak as much as possible for themselves. This method, of course, can produce scrap-heaps of quotation, but such a result will occur only if the assembler of material is undiscriminating in selection or unimaginative in presentation. Accordingly, in Chapter II, in which Shakespearean points of view are set forth, an attempt has been made to provide a running account which communicates elements of feeling as well as fact, and to insert into this account where it would lend most clarity and evocative effect the Shakespearean passages which best express the theme. As a result, it is hoped that one will enter upon interpretation not only with an awareness of ideas present in Shakespeare but also with a feeling for the emotional response to these ideas which an audience underwent as a scene or episode was played. Similarly, in Chapter IV, in which background materials are presented, care has been exercised to choose spokesmen valuable both for the typical data they furnish and for the way in which they express it. These men have been allowed to speak for themselves when they are most interesting, but their more pedestrian statements have been summarized. Pains have

[8] One way, that is, in a book like the present one, which is necessarily limited in scope. Under conditions more free the social interpreter of literature would do well to enter the field of "pure" criticism and show, not by argument, but by example, that techniques of art themselves can be interesting when related to cultural elements imposed by societies controlling authors, on the one hand, and critics, on the other. The "new criticism" should be valued for timely emphasis of artistic means to Shakespearean ends, and its characteristic concern with patterns of imagery, for example, can be amplified by the social critic through integration of some of these patterns with ideological traits, peculiar to the age, which Elizabethan plays exhibit. If, as Miss Spurgeon showed, the presiding image in *Hamlet* is the human body in sickness and disease, there is a plausible relation of this to the endless Elizabethan analogy between body and state. Something *was* rotten in the state of Denmark. There are some who will consider such issues precious and others who may consider them stodgy, but Elizabethan playwrights were very much concerned with disordered or "sick" societies and built many of their plays around that concept to a degree not yet generally understood.

been taken, however, lest this endeavor to be interesting should result in emotional exaggeration. Finally, there has been an attempt to make the historical data as readable as they can be made, and to this end Elizabethan spelling and punctuation have been modernized wherever clarity could be improved without impairment of strict meaning. The heaviness of Elizabethan prose disappears to a surprising degree when such purely mechanical blocks to communication are removed.

Common to studies of literature in relation to society there is still another evil, which is more difficult to avoid than those just reviewed. It is what may be called the fetish of consecutiveness. There is something disheartening, if not preposterous, about the way in which we often divide the consciousness of a poet, playwright, or novelist into compartments called "Politics," "Religion," "Psychology," or "Ethics," and then present each remnant of the dissected consciousness in a form equally artificial. This practice is generally one of presenting the subject's attitude toward politics, for example, along with a running gloss of pronouncements by his contemporaries. The conclusion follows, of course, that the author in question was expressing certain ideas of his time. Without denying the value of contributions made by this method, we may doubt its effectiveness in accounting for creative imagination. Someone should parody the formula by using it to explain a modern writer. Select Aldous Huxley; begin a chapter called "Economic Decentralization"; quote volubly from the author's Mr. Propter upon the subject; and follow this by fifty pages which illustrate what everyone from Thoreau to Justice Brandeis has uttered upon the evils of an overly complex society. Thus would the perverse, quixotic, and subtle Propter and his equally strange creator be "related to their times." More than a few historians have said that history is not a social science, but one of the humanities, and the factor most needed in the humanities is recognition of the complexities, the subtleties, and the rarities which go to make up individuality. Ironically enough, however, critics and scholars who most fear a lapse of literary study into social science are likely to be the very ones who produce consecutive and partitioned studies of authors in relation to milieu and environment. Some very nonliterary people could tell us that this method is inflexible and has been outmoded for some time.

The problem just discussed has been uncomfortably prominent in the preparation of this book, and it is probable that no very successful solution of it has been achieved. For one thing, the interpretation of Shakespearean plays and dramatic episodes which deal with the populace has become so involved that if thoroughness and fairness are to be manifested at all, attitudes contrary to the ones formulated must be set up with accuracy and then met by argument. Such a state of affairs hardly contributes to grace and expansiveness; instead, it invites the issue-by-issue discussion so productive of distortion in traditional scholarship. It is hoped that attempts at orderly consideration will not suggest that the writer believes difficult questions can be settled by pigeon-holing or "clear" definition. Every effort has been made to avoid this, so that no one will be led to think the problem can be divided into factors on the one hand religious and on the other material, or on one side political and on the other economic. Above all, in such a field as this it is unwise to attempt separation of logical from emotional concomitants, for thought and feeling in Elizabethan times were as forthrightly merged as they are in modern social controversy.

Thus far considered have been some restrictions which social interpreters of literature could voluntarily recognize. Equally important, however, is an affirmative obligation to be assumed: the analyst of social forces in literature ought to have a well-developed social philosophy, and he should be humble enough to know that such a philosophy cannot be attained by "common sense" of a stereotyped or insouciant nature. Social questions suffer unduly from this kind of simplification, which when orthodox often passes for soundness. One is reminded here of the recent objection to a book [9] which demonstrated that much Renaissance literary criticism proceeded from an aristocratic bias. The reviewer chose to question this by showing that many Renaissance literary critics were actually from the lower class and, moreover, that the aristocracy they manifested was an aristocracy, not of class, but of learning. Doubtless many will think his strictures cautious, sensible, and altogether judicious. What he has done, however, is to cloud the whole issue, largely because his social thinking is innocent of two ideas which were implicit in the book he attacked: frequently the greatest pretensions to aristocratic standards are exhibited by ambitious non-aristocrats, and not infrequently has an aristocracy of learning been a rationalization of class distinction. Knowing such things requires a modicum of worldliness and a modicum of the ability to detect social bias in unlikely places. The requirement that writers on social aspects of literature realize facts of this sort is not at all different from the requirement that historians of the religious aspects of literature know a little of the intricacies of religious attitudes and motives.

In addition to assuming an obligation of political awareness, the historian of social themes in literature might do well to disclose relevant portions of his social philosophy. Such a formulation will be good for him and very helpful to others, for impartiality on social issues, whether of the present or of the past, is an illusion. This is no defense of bigotry or of concealed propaganda; it is in fact the opposite, a recommendation that the critic explain his frame of reference so that both he and his readers will be more aware that contrary inferences are possible. As for the Shakespear-

[9] Vernon Hall, Jr., *Renaissance Literary Criticism* (New York, Columbia University Press, 1945). The criticism of it appears in *Studies in English* (The University of Texas, 1945–46), pp. 72 ff.

ean problem, it is interesting that obligation to disclose bias
rests more heavily upon "dispassionate" critics than upon
those who have an axe to grind. There can be no confusion,
for example, about Walt Whitman's militant democracy as a
basis for his earlier interpretation of Shakespeare, nor can
there be much question about the underlying premises of
Hazlitt or of Tolstoy. Ironically, however, much unconscious distortion has come from the very people who have
condemned Whitman, Hazlitt, Tolstoy, and others for prejudiced interpretation and have tried, laudably enough, to
understand Shakespeare, not to judge him. A good deal of
this misunderstanding might have been avoided had these
critics revealed their premises in prefatory statements. Some
might have disclosed their belief that democratic attitudes
are measurable, not by one's feeling toward groups or masses
of people, but by one's feeling toward individuals. Others
might have warned us that from the irrelevancy of judging
Shakespeare's work by the democratic views of our time they
had inferred that no issues of democracy were present in
Shakespeare's age. Still others could have announced as a
premise that social views implied by an author of the past
are evoked less by conflicts within society than by the social
attitudes of contemporary authors. An additional group of
critics could have declared frankly that when a playwright
takes over the social bias already present in his sources, his
own bias is not consciously operative and therefore is without
social significance. And more than one interpreter might have
warned us of his belief that because social ideas in literature
are expressed primarily in terms of character the only relevant question which arises is the character delineation which
such ideas help to achieve.

With reference to the problem at hand, these assumptions
could be expanded to fill a dozen pages. Anyone who has tried
to understand the ways in which writers work with ideas or to
fathom the vagaries of readers or audiences in responding to

them will be ready to protest the validity of all the premises which have just been reviewed. More than that, he will be disturbed by the ease with which these implicit attitudes pass as good currency and by the unconscious favoring of political quiescence, not to say conservatism, which most of them exhibit. Examination of the manner in which inarticulate premises have influenced interpretation will be undertaken in another chapter. The conclusion here is merely that brief formulation of them by their adherents would have warned readers of Shakespeare criticism that something was being assumed which was not one of the verities. And much more effective than brief formulation would have been genuine development of such assumptions with the intention of inviting self-analysis and critical response from others.

After suggesting that interpreters of social and political trends in literature owe to themselves and their readers a clear disclosure of bias upon the theme in question, it is up to the present interpreter to make his own disclosure. I believe that most of the benefits which one enjoys in a democratic society have been looked upon at one time or another as intrusions upon the natural order of things. I further believe that the most common method of resisting democratic reforms has been to associate them with destructive leveling, impiety, fantastic Utopianism, and disregard of cultural values. I do not believe, however, that all things so labeled have been potential reforms. I believe that the conflict of class versus mass is likely to characterize any age, and I look with suspicion upon claims that this or that period was one of real stability. I grant that the spread of political, cultural, and material benefits has been and will be accompanied by vulgarity, corruption, and injustice; I do not blame sensitive people for being alarmed at this, but I do think it is short-sighted and quixotic to respond mainly to these evil aspects of social evolution. Shaw's conclusion that democratic extension of culture must begin by popular preference for the

Illustrated London News rather than for the Kelmscott Chaucer [10] seems to me unpleasant but inescapable. But I dislike banality and mass standards and do not consider them to be automatically productive of something better. Nor do I think that one class of society is more responsible than another for the incidence of these things.

The foregoing credo, which is certainly not very original, is related to the material of this book because it has guided interpretation of a body of Elizabethan literature in which the populace has generally been depicted as illiterate, disorderly, and vicious. The task has been to relate this literary phenomenon to some of the social factors which produced it, particularly to a view of the populace which Elizabethan publicists sought to make current and applied repeatedly to a growing faction of society which finally rose against the monarchy in 1642. If Shakespeare is found occasionally to have lent himself to this, it does not follow that he was a propagandist in any outright sense of the term. Nor will it mean that more than one aspect of a many-sided dramatist is in question. Particularly, it will not mean that Shakespeare's artistry or humanity is to be impugned, except to those, either of the right or the left, to whom this question is so disturbing or absorbing that it cannot be considered without loss of perspective. It ought to mean simply that Shakespeare and others were caught in a movement of circumstances which they reflected in a manner some people of today find interesting as well as instructive.

[10] In the Preface to *Major Barbara.*

CHAPTER II

The Plays

THE ISSUE of democracy as Shakespeare faced it
emerges from three plays, *2 Henry VI* (the Cade
scenes), *Julius Caesar,* and *Coriolanus.* While most
readers will be familiar with these plays, few or none will
have read them all recently enough to retain the clear rec-
ollection which is necessary for adequate discussion. It is
probable, moreover, that many will have read them with
little concern for the political theme to which attention is
here directed. For these reasons a brief account of each will
be helpful, with special emphasis upon Shakespeare's treatment of the populace. Before an attempt at interpretation, a
description of the source materials from which the three plays
were derived will likewise be of assistance.

THE CADE SCENES

Scenes of the Cade rebellion, the fantastic and intense
episode in Act IV of *2 Henry VI,*[1] begin at Blackheath with
a colloquy between George Bevis and John Holland, who
inform us that "Jack Cade the clothier means to dress the
commonwealth, and turn it, and set a new nap on it." Thence,
after some ribaldry between them about their leader's doubt-
ful ancestry and well-flogged past, Cade, who has entered
with "Dick Butcher, Smith the Weaver, and a Sawyer, with
infinite numbers," recites his social objectives with the
farcical idealism traditional in antidemocratic satire. When
Cade is king, "the three hoop'd pot shall have ten hoops," it

[1] The Cade episode runs from Scene 2 to Scene 10.

shall be felony to drink small beer, the realm shall be held in common, and all shall be appareled in one livery. Lawyers shall die, for in Cade's words, "I did but seal once to a thing, and I was never mine own man since." Later, in Scene 6, as Cade sits on London-stone he commands at the city's cost that the conduit "run nothing but claret the first year of our reign," and in Scene 7 he orders all records of the realm to be burned; "My mouth," he declares, "shall be the parliament of England." Then, lest the economic side of his leveling program be forgotten, Cade reasserts it: "And henceforward all things shall be in common."

Melodramatic action accompanies this statement of lofty policies; the clerk of Chatham is dragged in, and because he can write his name he is ordered hanged with his pen and ink horn about his neck, just as Lord Say, in Scene 7, is sent to execution because, among other things, he "most traitorously corrupted the youth of the realm in erecting a grammar school" and kept men about him "that usually talk of a noun and a verb, and such abominable words as no Christian ear can endure to hear." When the lopped heads of Say and Cromer are brought in later, Cade commands: "Let them kiss one another, for they lov'd well when they were alive. Now part them again, lest they consult about the giving up of some more towns in France." By this time Cade has attained rank, for he has knighted himself by kneeling and saying, "Rise up Sir John Mortimer"; thus may he meet Sir Humphrey Stafford on equal terms.

At the opening of Scene 8 the "rabblement" is in full cry, and as it surges about him Cade bellows, "Up Fish Street! down Saint Magnus' corner! Throw them into Thames!" But a parley is suddenly sounded; Buckingham and Clifford enter attended, and thirteen lines later in an absurd anticlimax the mob, which is offered amnesty, is shouting, "God save the King! God save the King!" Fourteen more lines, and Cade has regained their tempestuous allegiance: "We'll follow Cade, we'll follow Cade!" Nineteen lines of denunciation from Clifford, and the mob is again loyal, shortly afterward to re-enter as "multitudes, with halters about their necks." At their final defection, Cade, in a rueful aside, speaks that endless formula of Elizabethan politics, "Was ever feather so lightly blown to and fro as this multitude?"

As traditionally interpreted, the function of this episode is largely limited to comic relief, as though comic relief and stern moralizing were mutually exclusive. To say that the scenes are comic is, of course, to understate the case, for as farce they are the work of a virtuoso. But there is more to be said of them than this, and it is said in the play itself. Spaced strategically among plebeian yawps and riot are choral commentaries leveled at the mob by the high-born *dramatis personae*. The Lord Say, "whose cheeks are pale for watching" over the common man's good, pleads with a humble dignity that Cade have mercy, "Whom have I injured that ye seek my death? . . . O let me live!" [2] The scene is intended to present an outrage upon humility, and Cade is touched with brief remorse as he orders Say's execution. Not so patient and pathetic as Say is Stafford, with his command "Rebellious hinds, the filth and scum of Kent, marked for the gallows, lay your weapons down"; [3] and lest the audience forget its lesson, the words of Alexander Iden as he kills Cade are intended to sober any groundling inclined to frivolity. In Scene 10 Iden is discovered musing in his garden.

> Lord! who would live turmoiled in the court
> And may enjoy such quiet walks as these?
> This small inheritance my father left me
> Contenteth me, and worth a monarchy.[4]
> I seek not to wax great by others' [waning],
> Or gather wealth, I care not with what envy: [5]
> Sufficeth that I have maintains my state
> And sends the poor well pleased from my gate.

[2] Act IV, scene 7, ll. 107–110. All references are those of the New Cambridge text, edited by Neilson and Hill.   [3] Act IV, scene 2, ll. 130–131.
[4] The line seems verbally confused.   [5] This line also seems unclear.

The gentle Iden then discovers Cade and is challenged by
the starving fugitive. "Nay," is the reply, "it shall never be
said . . . that Alexander Iden, an esquire of Kent, took
odds to combat a poor famished man." *Noblesse oblige.* But
Cade persists, is killed by Iden in self-defense, and makes
known his identity in a last whimsical boast. Here is the
gentle Iden now: [6]

> How much thou wrong'st me, heaven be my judge.
> Die, damned wretch, the curse of her that bare thee;
> And as I thrust thy body in with my sword,
> So wish I, I might thrust thy soul to hell.
> Hence will I drag thee headlong by the heels
> Unto a dunghill which shall be thy grave,
> And there cut off thy most ungracious head;
> Which I will bear in triumph to the King,
> Leaving thy trunk for crows to feed upon.

SOURCES OF THE CADE SCENES

It is well known that Shakespeare confused the chronicle
accounts of Cade's Rebellion with those of the Peasants'
Revolt in 1381 and that this confusion probably arose from
motives both of political emphasis and dramatic license. In
any event the accounts of the two uprisings, separated historically by seventy years, were merged by Shakespeare into
one episode. The Holinshed material thus used by Shakespeare was assembled years ago by Boswell-Stone, and its
presentation here is based largely upon his rendition,[7] with
selection confined to details of resemblance and difference
between play and source which suggest political emphasis.

Most of the violence and outrage in Shakespeare's version of the Cade uprising came from the chronicle story of
the earlier Peasants' Revolt. In that rebellion, according to

---

[6] It should be observed that the sudden shift in Iden's temperament makes
him dramatically much more effective as a choral character.

[7] W. G. Boswell-Stone, *Shakespeare's Holinshed* (New York, Longmans,
Green and Company, 1896).

Holinshed, Wat Tyler demanded death for all lawyers,[8] and the same authority likewise has it that in 1381 "it was dangerous among them [the rebels] to be known for one that was learned, and more dangerous if any man were found with a penner and inkhorn at his side." [9] Hence Cade's decision in Shakespeare's play to hang the clerk of Chatham "with his pen and inkhorn about his neck." Holinshed's version of the Peasants' Revolt, moreover, contains the exhortation of John Ball for slaughter of the lords and gentry, together with the observation: "for so might they [the peasants] procure peace and surety to themselves in time to come, if, dispatching out of the way the great men, there should be an equality in liberty, no difference in degrees of nobility, but a like dignity and equal authority in all things brought in among them." [10] Cade's directions in Shakespeare's version, "Go some and pull down the Savoy; others to th' Inns of Court, down with them all," come likewise from the chronicled events of 1381: "Now after that these wicked people had thus destroyed the Duke of Lancaster's house and done what they could devise to his reproach, they went to the temple, and burnt the men of law's lodgings . . . and all that they might lay hand upon." [11] Similarly, Cade's decision that the laws of England shall issue from his mouth and his order to burn the records of the realm are clearly referable to Holinshed's description of the earlier rebellion. Wat Tyler proclaimed, "putting his hands to his lips, that within four days all the laws of England should come forth of his mouth." [12] So Holinshed relates it, and in another passage he writes that the rebels of 1381 "purposed to burn and destroy all records, evidences, court rolls, and other monuments." [13]

Such are the historical details of 1381 which Shakespeare transferred to Cade's uprising of 1450. There are, however,

[8] *Ibid.*, p. 271. In notes 9–15 the numbers refer to pages in *Shakespeare's Holinshed.* The reader may check with Holinshed by using the reference provided in each case by Boswell-Stone. [9] Page 272 (see note 8, above). [10] *Ibid.* [11] Page 277. [12] Page 278. [13] *Ibid.*

two acts of violence in Shakespeare's episode which were taken, not from the chronicle account of the Peasants' Revolt, but from the chronicle story of Cade. In Shakespeare, Cade's order "to break open the gaols, and let out the prisoners" draws authority from Holinshed's version in which the rebel, "for making him more friends, broke up the gaols of the King's Bench and Marshalsea." [14] And Holinshed likewise ascribes to Cade the beheading of Say and Cromer, together with the sequel to it: "and with these two heads this bloody wretch entered into the city again, and as it were in a spite caused them in every street to kiss together, to the great detestation of all the beholders." [15] Plainly, however, the breaking of the jails and the macabre pageant of the heads was not impressive enough for Shakespeare, who drew the bulk of the outrage in his episode from the account of events in 1381.

It is in his ascription to Cade of stupidity and clumsiness, however, that Shakespeare actually runs counter to the chronicles. Far from being the ridiculous equalitarian and Utopian that Shakespeare makes of him, the Holinshed Cade is "a young man of goodly stature and right pregnant wit," "sober in talk, wise in reasoning, arrogant in heart, and stiff in opinion." [16] In Southwark his conduct was that of "prohibiting to all his retinue murder, rape, and robbery; by which color of well meaning, he the more allured him to the hearts of the common people." [17] "Open rapine and manifest robbery," however, ensue in Holinshed after Cade's entry into London.[18] There is, of course, no sympathy or admiration for revolutionists in the chronicle, but the demands of the Kentish rebels are listed fairly and completely. The "Complaint of the Commons of Kent" [19] sets forth fifteen specific grievances, typical among which are allegations that the king is surrounded by new ministers, "mean persons of a

---

[14] Page 273.   [15] Page 279.
[16] Holinshed, *Chronicles* (London, 1808), III, 220 and 224.
[17] *Ibid.*, p. 224.   [18] *Ibid.*, p. 225.   [19] *Ibid.*, pp. 222–223.

lower nature," and thereby is kept from hearing complaints of the common people; that excessive taxation and extortion are practiced against the commons; and that the people of Kent are prevented from choosing knights of the shire by free election. As given in Holinshed, the "Requests by the Captain of the Great Assembly in Kent" [20] are petitions simply that the king may really rule, that traitors to the cause of good government be executed, and that extortion be stopped. Holinshed declares indeed that the council considered these requests "proud and presumptuous," but he makes no attempt to suppress their public-spirited character or to conceal their moderate nature. Shakespeare ignores these matters completely, and ascribes to Cade the program of preposterous reform which has been reviewed.

Another interesting change by Shakespeare prejudicial to Cade is the dramatist's calculated choice of Hall's version of Cade's death in preference to that of Holinshed. It will be recalled that in Shakespeare the peaceful Iden, musing in his garden, is surprised by Cade and forced to kill in self-defense. It is because of Iden's innocent and pacific qualities before this fight that his subsequent moral fury in Shakespeare becomes so impressive, and Shakespeare evidently selected Hall's version to lay the foundation for this, for in Holinshed, Iden (Eden) deliberately awaits Cade, hoping to collect the price which has been placed on the latter's head. In Hall this mercenary motive is lacking; other details, such as the name "Iden" instead of "Eden" and the reference to Iden as an "esquire of Kent," confirm Shakespeare's use of Hall instead of Holinshed for this last part of the Cade episode.[21]

JULIUS CAESAR

In *Julius Caesar* the self-interest and sorry instability of the Roman populace turn the tide against Brutus and the

[20] *Ibid.*, pp. 223–224.
[21] See the discussion of this by Lucille King, *Philological Quarterly*, XIII (1934), 325.

other conspirators. Although their ill fortune materializes at Philippi, the climactic change from good to ill for the conspirators occurs in Act III with the shift against them of mob sentiment. Accordingly, it will not surprise those familiar with Shakespeare's methods of exposition that the note of plebeian stupidity and mutability is struck powerfully in the opening scene of the play. There the disorderly citizens, who have decked themselves in their best "to make holiday, to see Caesar and to rejoice in his triumph," are denounced by their own tribunes for ingratitude and change of heart. After the cynical speech by Marullus on the crowd's erstwhile devotion to Caesar's adversary, Flavius pronounces chorally upon its exit:

> See, whether their basest metal be not moved;
> They vanish tongue-tied in their guiltiness.

The next we hear of the Roman mob is from Casca who, in the well-known lines of Scene 2, reports its reception of Caesar's refusal of the crown.

. . . and still as he refus'd it, the rabblement hooted and clapp'd their chapp'd hands and threw up their sweaty nightcaps and uttered such a deal of stinking breath because Caesar refus'd the crown, that it had almost choked Caesar, for he swounded and fell down at it; and for mine own part, I durst not laugh, for fear of opening my lips and receiving the bad air.

Casca ends his splenetic account of the populace with the "three or four wenches, where I stood" who cried "Alas, good soul!" and one is reminded of Richard II on Bolingbroke's courtship of the people: "Off goes his bonnet to an oyster wench." Both Richard and Casca are jaundiced personalities, and their allusions to humanity in the mass are doubtless in character and part of the characterization process. As discussion progresses, however, it will be observed that Shakespeare generally uses characters of a cynically patrician humor for comment upon the populace and that a dramatist's calculation of audience response may be largely revealed by such consistent choice of commentators. Moreover, when the "slanting" is not done by aristocrats, when it is done by the tribunes in the present play, and by Cade's own followers or indeed by Cade himself in *2 Henry VI,* the picture drawn of popular assemblage is altogether as scurrilous.

The next appearance of the citizenry is in the second scene of Act III. After the killing of Caesar in the previous scene, Brutus and Cassius enter with a throng of citizens who are given the first line, "We will be satisfied; let us be satisfied." The citizens divide, some to hear Cassius, others to hear Brutus. The honest and highly epigrammatic speech of Brutus quickly converts the suspicious crowd, and they clamor, "Let him be Caesar"; "Caesar's better parts shall be crown'd in Brutus." The uproar of impulsive approval is so loud that Brutus must implore silence so that Antony may speak, and as Antony goes into the pulpit there are cries, " 'Twere best he speak no harm of Brutus here" and "This Caesar was a tyrant."

Antony's speech need not be reviewed, but the mass response to it and, above all, Antony's opportunistic gauging and manipulation of that response are factors in the problem which require attention. In complete contrast with Brutus, Antony is no expounder but rather an evoker who pulls, one by one and each at the strategic moment, all the stops of the organ. Some forty lines following a self-effacing start, his nostalgic reminiscences of Caesar and his apparent emotional breakdown have the citizens murmuring in his favor. His mention of Caesar's will and quick disavowal of intent to read it increase the murmur to a clamor, in the midst of which he produces Caesar's bloody mantle; the clamor then becomes a frenzy as the citizenry cry, "About! Seek! Burn! Fire! Kill! Slay!" Caesar's wounds, "poor dumb mouths" are given tongues as the mob is tensed to the critical pitch.

In their upheaval the commoners forget the will, and Antony, with what seems cold-blooded cynicism, calls them back to hear Caesar's bequests in their favor. After that there is no check which can be put on them as they rush through the city with firebrands; significantly enough, they accomplish only irrelevant violence in killing Cinna the poet who, for want of a better reason, is torn for his bad verses.

THE SOURCE OF *Julius Caesar*

In his chapter on the source of *Julius Caesar*, M. W. MacCallum [22] is not specifically concerned with Shakespeare's presentation of Rome's unreasonable populace. At the outset, however, he does discuss the peculiar shiftiness of the mob's bullying questions addressed to the poet Cinna. MacCallum observes that none of this is in Plutarch and that it is Shakespeare's realistic contribution based upon intuitive understanding of the behavior of bravoes who have run down a victim. [23] This is valuable. As a short scene in which the bland sadistic stare and the irrelevant retort are thrust upon an innocent who tries to explain himself, the episode deserves more space than MacCallum devotes to it. In its forty lines are packed such an awareness of the hostility and cogent unreason found in class conflict that the scene could be called modern in all senses, sober and ironical, of the term. For in Shakespeare's conception there is surely none of the wistful expectation that aroused masses will act objectively; the scene rests upon a knowledge of such behavior in crisis which is hard to explain other than by the dramatist's intuitive observation.

While he comments briefly upon this bit of realism as a factor not found in Shakespeare's source, MacCallum is silent

[22] *Shakespeare's Roman Plays and Their Background* (London, The Macmillan Company, 1925), pp. 187 ff. The information furnished by MacCallum relating to the problem at hand is very general. A collateral issue of interest is his discussion of the change in Shakespeare of Brutus' attitude toward monarchy. [23] *Ibid.*, p. 198.

upon a similiar and far more elaborate transmutation of source material. It is well known that the speeches of Brutus and Antony in the funeral scene are Shakespeare's own, but no discussion of altered sources would be adequate which failed to note the political realism which underlies these additions. From Plutarch Shakespeare certainly derived Brutus's high-mindedness and his tactical error in allowing Antony to speak,[24] but there is no implication, in the source, of the kind of speech Brutus made. It has the laconic and functional sparseness of the Gettysburg Address. Tragically, however, it is not delivered as a tribute to men who died in battle, but as justification of a political *coup* and as an appeal for mass support. Shakespeare conceives of Brutus as an idealist who believes that facts honestly and simply explained are politically adequate. Because of his concern not to sully himself and his pains to represent his opposition fairly, Brutus wins support only until Antony begins to explore crowd responses. And although Shakespeare may not have intended it, Brutus's speech exhibits perfectly the egocentrism of those who make a religion of objectivity. The scorn of emotionality suggested by it, the conviction implied in it that orderly analysis is pre-eminent, and the perfectionistic compactness of it as a composition, all suggest a self-regard by the inward eye which may be the bliss of solitude, but which is fatal in an emergency requiring audience response.

Antony's famous rejoinder is a *tour de force* which completes Shakespeare's picture of the kind of persuasion most effective with the citizenry. Plutarch does give the prescription for this speech, but only in formula. "When [Antony] saw that the people were very glad and desirous also to hear Caesar spoken of, and his praises uttered, he mingled his oration with lamentable words, and by amplifying of matters did greatly move their hearts and affections." [25]

[24] *Shakespeare's Plutarch,* ed. by Tucker Brooke (London, Chatto and Windus, 1909), I, 137.   [25] *Ibid.,* II, 22.

The gist of this is the essence of Antony's oration. Antony, above all, is an analyst of audience temper; he first finds what his listeners want to hear and then wanders among the by-paths of their "hearts and affections." Shakespeare's grasp of crowd psychology has been the subject of study,[26] but there remains a need to examine Antony's speech for its surprising arsenal of cynical devices. There is the vivid and platitudinous beginning:

> The evil that men do lives after them;
> The good is oft interred with their bones.

Next comes the apparent admission against interest: "If it [Caesar's ambition] were so, it was a grievous fault." Now occurs a hint of the common touch, "When that the poor have cried, Caesar hath wept." Then, just as Antony is beginning to warm to his subject, comes his first exploratory halt; apparently inarticulate with emotion, he must pause till his heart, "in the coffin there with Caesar," comes back to him. The commoners begin to mutter and Antony, sensing it, advances to the next strategic point: he mentions Caesar's will but disclaims all intention of capitalizing upon material interest. Another exploratory pause, and as the citizens clamor for the will Antony knows that he can throw caution away. His subsequent move is to produce the concrete object, the evocative thing which men can touch and see, Caesar's gown with the bloody rents in it. But first he recalls old times and old campaigns.

> I remember
> The first time ever Caesar put it on;
> 'Twas on a summer's evening, in his tent
> That day he overcame the Nervii.

And now, in a climax of mingled sentiment and abuse, he holds the grisly thing up for the crowd to see. Next, and in clinching employment of the concrete objective device, he

[26] Frederick Tupper, "The Shakespearean Mob," *PMLA* XXVII (1912), 486–523.

drives the crowd's attention directly to the hacked body of Caesar, and there is no holding them. They even forget the will which Antony, who has saved material interest as the most telling and final point, must call them back to hear. This is not a pretty example of how to manipulate the electorate, and it is even less so when we perceive two ingredients which do not occur at any one point, but are pervasive. In contrast with the understatement of Brutus, who tells the crowd briefly why he killed his best friend, Antony's irony, with its six-fold repetition of the "honorable men" phrase, evolves steadily into the most blatant kind of sarcasm. He knows the inadequacy of quiet irony; he also knows the value of repetition and how to use it climactically. The second pervasive factor in Antony's speech is that the crowd really makes it for him. He could have learned nothing from a Dale Carnegie, for he knows with sure insight that he cannot really convince people unless they think they are convincing themselves or, better yet, that they are convincing him. He is "no orator, as Brutus is," but "just a plain blunt man" who is trying to think this thing out with the rest of them.

Shakespeare's penetration into this darker side of political behavior rivals two modern fictional efforts in that direction, both of them based in a nonliteral way upon the career of Huey Long.[27] Whether his cynical picture of mass persuasion is based upon intuition or observation or both, it is impossible to say. One thing is certain, however: the contributions of Plutarch to Shakespeare's conception of how the popular mind may be translated into action are limited to a skeletal formula with bare details concerning the will, the bloody gown, and Caesar's body.

In evaluating Shakespeare's use of Plutarch in this episode, we have not only the demagoguery of Antony's speech to consider but also a portrait of the populace itself. Concerning

[27] John Dos Passos, *Number One*, and Robert Penn Warren, *All the King's Men*.

the latter, the evidence is conflicting. As the account in Plutarch is followed, it would seem at first that Shakespeare had made a gratuitous and major change in order to emphasize the instability of crowd responses. All readers of Shakespeare know that in his play the citizenry plumps solidly for Brutus, only to change over suddenly at Antony's provocation. Plutarch's account of Marcus Brutus, however, runs entirely counter to this.

When the people saw him [Brutus] in the pulpit, although they were a multitude of rakehells of all sorts, and had a good will to make some stir: yet being ashamed to do it for the reverence they bare unto Brutus, they kept silence to hear what he would say. When Brutus began to speak, they gave him quiet audience: *howbeit immediately after, they showed that they were not at all contented with the murder.* For when another called Cinna [the conspirator] would have spoken, and began to accuse Caesar, they fell into a great uproar among them and marvelously reviled him.[28]

The account of the same event in Plutarch's life of Caesar depicts the citizenry as being moved by Brutus neither one way nor the other.[29]

There are two reasons, however, why this change taken by itself cannot be relied upon to show a transmutation by Shakespeare with intention of casting discredit upon the populace. The first of these is that there is dramatic reason for the change: it is simply more effective to show a populace swayed first one way and then the other, and the story would be flat without it. Perhaps this principle, if extended, would also account, upon a purely dramatic basis, for the cynical virtuosity exhibited in Antony's speech. Indeed, examination will be made shortly of the too frequently accepted theory that Shakespeare's changes of source are good evidence of doctrinal emphasis on his part. A second reason why little can be made of Shakespeare's change in this episode is that although Plutarch does not exhibit a fickle citizenry first in agreement with Brutus and immediately afterward with Antony, he does elsewhere and generally give clear hints of its instability. In the life of Marcus Brutus, and but a few pages beyond the excerpt just quoted, occurs this description of the populace just after Antony's winning of their favor: "The people growing weary now of Antonius' pride and insolency, who ruled all things in manner with absolute power: they desired that Brutus might return again." [30]

Beyond the specific data described in the last few pages, there are some general notions in Plutarch which bear upon the problem and find their way into Shakespeare's adaptation of the episode. There is material throughout which establishes the opportunistic allegiance of the populace to Caesar. Cato, for example, feared "insurrection of the poor needy persons, which were they that put all their hope in Caesar." [31] Caesar, moreover, "began to put forth laws meeter for a seditious Tribune than for a Consul: because by them he preferred the division of lands, and the distributing of corn to every citizen, *gratis*, to please them withal." [32] The people are described, however, as antagonistic to the idea of Caesar as emperor, and as making outcries of joy when he refused the crown.[33] And in direct line with Shakespeare's conception of a Rome plagued with popular insurrection, we learn from Plutarch that

Rome itself also was immediately filled with the flowing repair of all the people their neighbors thereabouts, which came hither from all parties like droves of cattle, that there was neither officer nor magistrate that could any more command them by authority, neither by any persuasion of reason bridle such a confused and disorderly multitude: so that Rome had in manner destroyed itself for lack of rule and order.[34]

Plutarch, in fact, declares that "men of deep judgment and learning" were so concerned with the "fury and madness" of the people that they "thought themselves happy if the

[30] *Ibid.*, p. 139.   [31] *Ibid.*, p. 12.   [32] *Ibid.*, p. 19.
[33] *Ibid.*, pp. 90, 91, 93.   [34] *Ibid.*, p. 52.

commonwealth were no worse troubled than with the absolute state of a monarchy and sovereign lord to govern
them." [35] Unlike his story of Coriolanus, Plutarch's account
of Caesar, and to some extent his story of Brutus, provided
Shakespeare with a ready-made aversion to the populace
which amounts to contempt. Apparently unnoticed by source
studies, which have been more concerned with story and
characterization than with social bias, is a brief passage in
the life of Marcus Brutus which probably furnished the cue
for Shakespeare's opening scene. This scene is begun by
Flavius with a denunciation of the commoners, containing
the line, "What! know you not, being mechanical. . . ." In
the scene, moreover, six of the seven responses from the citizenry are made by a cobbler. The suggestion for this may
well have been words in Plutarch addressed by Cassius to
Brutus: *"What! knowest thou not* that thou art Brutus?
Thinkest thou that they be *cobblers,* tapsters, or suchlike base
mechanical people, that write these bills and scrolls. . . ?" [36]
Whether the passage suggested part of Shakespeare's opening scene or not, it is typical of the social point of view toward
commoners which was available to Shakespeare in his source
data.

Finally, in a source-play comparison involving *Julius
Caesar* it should be made plain that Plutarch supplied Shakespeare with the flagrant and literally inflammatory action of
the mob which follows Antony's oration.

But when they had opened Caesar's testament and found a liberal
legacy of money bequeathed unto every citizen of Rome, and that they
saw his body (which was brought into the market place) all bemangled
with gashes of swords: then there was no order to keep the multitude
and common people quiet. . . . Then . . . they took the firebrands,
and went unto their houses that had slain Caesar, to set them afire.

[35] *Ibid.,* p. 45. MacCallum quotes this.
[36] *Ibid.,* p. 122. The italics are mine. The passage is not marked with dag-
gers which is the editor's manner of indicating passages which supplied
Shakespeare with both subject matter and wording. Nor is it marked with
asterisks, the method followed of indicating borrowed subject matter.

Others also ran up and down the city to see if they could meet with any of them, to cut them in pieces.[37]

Directly after this comes Plutarch's description of the mobbing of Cinna the poet.

CORIOLANUS

Unlike mobs in the Cade scenes or in *Julius Caesar*, the common citizenry in *Coriolanus* is given ample basis for discontent; it is also provided with notable provocation to resistance by the scurrility of the hero. Although in the opening lines one citizen proposes the killing of Caius Marcius, "chief enemy to the people," so that the plebs may have corn at their own price, yet in the demands of the people there is none of the evil farce present in Jack Cade's declarations. Aside from his appeal to violence, the First Citizen speaks in a standard pattern of sixteenth-century social protest.

We are accounted poor citizens, the patricians good. What authority surfeits on would relieve us. If they would yield us but the superfluity while it were wholesome, we might guess they relieved us humanely; but they think we are too dear: the leanness that afflicts us, the object of our misery, is as an inventory to particularize their abundance; our sufferance is a gain to them. Let us revenge this with our pikes, ere we become rakes; for the gods know I speak this in hunger for bread, not in thirst for revenge.[38]

And in the lines following, the wisdom and justice of reprisal against Caius Marcius are weighed carefully and with forbearance.

Sec. Cit. Would you proceed especially against Caius Marcius?
All. Against him first; he's a very dog to the commonalty.
Sec. Cit. Consider you what services he has done for his country?
First Cit. Very well; and could be content to give him good report for't, but that he pays himself with being proud.
Sec. Cit. Nay, but speak not maliciously.
First Cit. I say unto you, what he hath done famously, he did it to that end. Though soft-conscienced men can be content to say it was for

[37] *Ibid.*, p. 104.   [38] Act I, scene 1, ll. 16–25.

his country, he did it to please his mother, and to be partly proud;
which he is, even to the altitude of his virtue.

Sec. Cit. What he cannot help in his nature, you account a vice in him.
You must in no way say he is covetous.

After the entry of Menenius, whom the Second Citizen
calls "one that hath always loved the people," Shakespeare
actually provides for a powerful and dignified popular manifesto. Of the patricians, whom Menenius has been praising
for their "most charitable care," a citizen retorts:

Care for us! True, indeed! They ne'er car'd for us yet: suffer us to
famish, and their store-houses crammed with grain; make edicts for
usury, to support usurers; repeal daily any wholesome act established
against the rich, and provide more piercing statutes daily, to chain up
and restrain the poor. If the wars eat us not up, they will; and there's
all the love they bear us.[39]

Even as Menenius is about to answer this as "wondrous
malicious" or else folly, the same citizen observes of Menenius' proposed fable, "Well, I'll hear it, sir; yet you must not
think to fob off our disgrace with a tale; but, an't please you,
deliver." Then comes from Menenius the well-known fable
of the belly and the members, which is choral material of the
same stamp as Ulysses' speech upon degree in *Troilus and
Cressida.* There was a time when the body's members rebelled
against the belly, "idle and unactive, still cupboarding the
viand, never bearing like labour with the rest." How did the
"cormorant belly" answer the mutinous members? It smiled,
and Menenius seems in some sort of pantomime to mimic the
belly smiling—it smiled and reminded the malcontents that it,
"the store-house and shop of the whole body," serves to
nourish all else which "from me do back receive the flour of
all, and leave me but the bran." To the question, "How apply
you this?" Menenius pronounces:

> The senators of Rome are this good belly,
> And you the mutinous members; for examine

[39] *Ibid.,* ll. 81–89.

> Their counsels and their cares, digest things rightly
> Touching the weal o' th' common, you shall find
> No public benefit which you receive
> But it proceeds or comes from them to you
> And no way from yourselves. What do you think,
> You, the great toe of this assembly?

The "great toe" thus addressed is the leader of the rebellion. Caius Marcius now enters with his ingratiating,

> What's the matter, you dissentious rogues,
> That rubbing the itch of your opinion,
> Make yourselves scabs?

At the ironical reply of the Second Citizen, "We have ever your good word," the stiff-necked patrician retaliates with some fifty lines of invective which makes good the promise of his quoted beginning. Curs, frightened in war and vain in peace, mutable as ice upon fire, kept from eating one another only by their masters, presumptuous meddlers in state affairs, quoters of fatuous proverbs "that hunger broke stone walls, that dogs must eat, that meat was made for mouths"—such are the citizens. The supreme contempt of Caius Marcius is saved for the last to accompany his announcement that "their vulgar wisdoms" have now been granted tribunes for their defense and "for insurrection's arguing." And as our patrician leaves to fight the Volsces, he contemptuously invites the citizenry to follow: "The Volsces have much corn; take these rats thither to gnaw their garners." In Scene 5 certain of the rats are indeed seen looting in Corioli, stealing among other things "doublets that hangmen would bury with those that wore them."

Act II brings together the irreconcilables. Caius Marcius, now Coriolanus, returns from victory, and to gain the consulship he must appear before the people wearing a gown of humility, exhibiting his wounds, and suing for political favor. Before the return of Coriolanus, however, an elaborate discussion of politics is carried on between Menenius and the two tribunes, Sicinius and Brutus. The tribunes talk of the unendurable pride of Coriolanus and are answered by Menenius:

> You talk of pride: O that you could turn your eyes toward the napes of your necks, and make but an interior survey of your good selves! O that you could!
>
> *Both.* What then, sir?
>
> *Men.* Why, then you should discover a brace of unmeriting, proud, violent, testy magistrates, alias fools, as any in Rome.
>
> *Sic.* Menenius, you are known well enough too.[40]

Menenius shortly dismisses the two representatives of the people.

> Our very priests must become mockers, if they shall encounter such ridiculous subjects as you are. When you speak best unto the purpose, it is not worth the wagging of your beards; and your beards deserve not so honourable a grave as to stuff a botcher's cushion, or to be entombed in an ass's pack-saddle. Yet you must be saying Marcius is proud; who, in a cheap estimation, is worth all your predecessors since Deucalion, though peradventure some of the best of 'em were hereditary hangmen. God-den to your worships. More of your conversation would infect my brain, being the herdsmen of the beastly plebeians. I will be bold to take my leave of you.

Certain observations have traditionally been made about the objective and neutral character of Menenius, but by his own description he is one "known to be a humorous patrician, and one that loves a cup of hot wine with not a drop of allaying Tiber in it . . . hasty and tinder-like upon too trivial motion." [41] He is, however, a humor character designed for choral commentary: "What I think, I utter, and spend my malice in my breath"; and that what he thinks and what he utters is intended by Shakespeare as the truth about the populace is corroborated by the equally quixotic contempt for commoners uttered by one of their own number, the Third Citizen of Scene 3. The First Citizen has said that Coriolanus "stuck not to call us the many-headed multitude." To which the Third Citizen answers:

---

[40] Act II, scene 1, ll. 41–50.   [41] Act II, scene 1, ll. 51–55.

We have been called so of many, not that our heads are some brown, some black, some abram, some bald, but that our wits, are so diversely coloured; and truly I think if all our wits were to issue out of one skull, they would fly east, west, north, south, and their consent of one direct way should be at once to all the points o' tho' compass.

The struggle of Coriolanus with himself and with Menenius, as he stands "in this wolvish toge . . . to beg of Hob and Dick . . . their needless vouches," is a monument to wry slumming by patricians. By not behaving too intolerably he is accepted by the populace with that spastic enthusiasm which antidemocrats have traditionally believed to accompany all decisions made by popular assemblies. Then the familiar pattern is enacted; just as the mob roared for Brutus, only to do Antony's bidding immediately after, the citizenry here is led forthrightly by the tribunes into repealing its approval of Coriolanus.

Act III shows Coriolanus in as bad a light as that in which Act II exhibits the tribunes and the plebeians. Crossed by the tribunes after the popular shift against him, Caius Marcius blatantly speaks of the "mutable rank-scented many," publicly declares that any concession to the populace nourishes rebellion and calls one of the tribunes "this Triton of the minnows." His behavior is so outrageous that the tribunes order his arrest, and public disorder ensues in which Coriolanus draws on the aediles and is repeatedly rebuked by Menenius, ever at his side as a hopelessly unsuccessful mediator. Later, at the imploring of Volumnia and his friends who have well-founded fears for the safety of Rome, Coriolanus is induced to attempt a reconciliation. In the negotiation which follows, he is charged by one of the tribunes with conspiracy against popular government and with being a traitor. As he ignores the pleas of Menenius and flies into a rage, the citizens demand that he suffer death by being thrown from the Tarpeian rock. As the third act closes, he is sentenced to banishment and he meets this judgment with staggering vitupera-

tion concerning the stench, mutability, cowardice, and ignorance of the people. They in turn revel in his banishment,
with cries of Hoo! Hoo!

Act IV supplies the play's true political emphasis by that
most obvious and effective of all the means of dramatic commentary, the "tables turned" device, which will be discussed
later as a method of emphasis and audience orientation. It is
sufficient to note at this point that Scene 6 offers one of the
lustiest and most sustained situations in Shakespeare of a
group of characters confronted by their own folly. Here the
tribunes and citizenry are held solely responsible by Cominius
and Menenius for the ruin of Rome by Coriolanus' desertion
to the Volscians.

THE SOURCE OF *Coriolanus*

As with interpretation of *Julius Caesar*, a source study of
Coriolanus will be found interesting, but not conclusive, in
establishing the intended doctrinal emphasis of the play. In
the end we shall have to be content to infer doctrinal content
from some standard devices of dramatic emphasis which will
be considered in due course. For the sake of completeness,
however, there should be a review of the findings which Mac-
Callum derived from careful comparison of the play with
its sources.

MacCallum demonstrates that Shakespeare has converted
Plutarch's tribunes into a pair of demogogues [42] and has
made the populace both cowardly and witless.[43] Because of
this added ingredient of popular ineptitude, MacCallum believes that Shakespeare "has made the most momentous and
remarkable change in the story. . . ." "The grand characteristic which the Tudor Englishman rejects, or all but
rejects, is the intuitive political capacity which Plutarch, perhaps in idealizing retrospect, attributes to all classes of citizens in the young republic." [44] MacCallum also charges that

[42] *Shakespeare's Roman Plays*, p. 501.   [43] *Ibid.*, p. 530.
[44] *Ibid.*, pp. 517–518.

Shakespeare ignores social injustices which in Plutarch lead to unrest and to establishment of the tribunate. In Plutarch the senate has goaded the populace to desperation by refusing to check the scandalous practice of usurers in seizing not only the property but the persons of debtors, "notwithstanding all the wounds and cuts they showed, which they had received in many battles, fighting for the defense of their country and commonwealth." Many magistrates and senators have sided with the plebs, but Marcius has held out against them, not because he cares that creditors are losing money, but because he thinks lenity is the beginning of disobedience and that "the proud attempt of the commonalty was to abolish law and bring all to confusion." According to Plutarch, the mass action of the "poor common people" by which they gained the tribunate was merely that of walking out of the city, "offering no creature any hurt or violence, or making any show of actual rebellion." [45]

There is, however, another episode in Plutarch in which the tribunes, "busy prattlers," circulate the slander that the nobles had deliberately created a scarcity of corn. And it is this spurious grievance, to the exclusion of the one against usurers, which Shakespeare selects for motivation of his populace. Of the usury episode, "in which the younger contemporary of Nero favors the people," MacCallum observes that "the elder contemporary of Pym summarily dismisses [it], and substitutes for it another far less important, in which [the people] appear in no very creditable light." [46]

No one who has read the account of Coriolanus in North's Plutarch will disagree factually with MacCallum's considered comparisons. The question is one of interpretation. We may examine first the most serious charge: that Shakespeare has ignored the callous injustice of Marcius and the senate in refusing to redress grievances of the citizens, many of them disabled soldiers, against usurers and has substi-

[45] *Shakespeare's Plutarch,* II, 145. [46] *Shakespeare's Roman Plays,* p. 524.

tuted an episode in which the misled populace cries for bread and gets tribunes. In the first place, and parenthetically, the real villains of the Shakespearean story are the tribunes; witness the "tables turned" episode of Act IV, Scene 6, in which the whole force of consequences is turned against these officials. We can guess that Shakespeare had decided upon this emphasis and was naturally attracted to the corn episode in Plutarch because in it the tribunes play a shady part. The real point, however, as distinguished from the parenthetical one, is the change Shakespeare made. So far as his play is concerned, there is nothing spurious or trumped up about the corn shortage: the citizens have not been deceived by demagogues, as in Plutarch; they simply believe their social superiors are responsible. They not only believe this, but they offer at the play's very beginning a moving protest against it. MacCallum's charge that the motives of the populace have been perverted by selection of the corn episode ignores the favorable change Shakespeare made in it and would seem to rest finally upon a feeling that starvation is a less worthy motive for social action than exploitation by usurers.

There is further conjecture open, moreover, upon Shakespeare's choice of the food crisis as motivation. The statement of immediate cause for the corn shortage as it appears in North's Plutarch is that "the most part of the arable land within the territory of Rome was become heathy and barren for lack of ploughing." [47] There is a parallel between this state of affairs and that which lay behind the enclosure riots of 1607, which occasioned among other comment the noteworthy sermon of Robert Wilkinson, which will be discussed in a subsequent chapter. Not only are the corn shortage themes of Plutarch and Shakespeare analogous to the English situation, but these enclosure riots and the probable date of *Coriolanus* sufficiently coincide. Therefore Shakespeare, in his choice of the corn incident in Plutarch, could have been

[47] *Shakespeare's Plutarch*, II, 156.

influenced by its topical parallel with events of his own time. There remains MacCallum's general contention, previously cited, that Shakespeare's most momentous change in Plutarch's story was gratuitous ascription to the Roman citizenry of political incompetence. That this change was made and that it makes a great difference must be granted immediately by any reader of the two accounts, but the trouble comes in assuming that this over-all transformation can establish intention on Shakespeare's part to weight the play with a Jacobean conservative bias.

In checking this assumption we may analyze first a case or two in which change by Shakespeare of his source material is actually demonstrative of intended political emphasis. When the Bishop of Carlisle, at the moment of Bolingbroke's usurpation, is given lines prophesying that the blood of Englishmen shall manure the ground and future ages groan for the foul act, he does not speak as he does in the chronicles, but states instead a conventional sixteenth-century belief about the origins of pre-Tudor anarchy. There are no dramatic reasons for this change: the part of Carlisle's declaration drawn from the chronicles, that no subject may pass sentence upon a king, would have been sufficient; so the addition to it was probably made for doctrinal emphasis. Similarly, when Shakespeare, in using Arthur Brooke's poem, converts the basic emphasis of *Romeo and Juliet* to the Tudor doctrine that "civil blood makes civil hands unclean," the conversion of source may be presumed to have political emphasis as a motive. Here, again, the change cannot be accounted for by dramatic necessity or expediency.

There are also intermediate cases. In the Cade scenes, as already noted, the supernally banal program of social reform adopted by the rebels is not suggested by the chronicle account of Cade, but is a bawdy and harum-scarum rendition of ideas drawn from the chronicle version of the Peasants' Revolt. This change might be explained as merely dramatic because conceivably it is nothing more than provision for farce to lighten the heavy historical theme. What makes the case an intermediate one, however, is the principle that comic relief and political emphasis are not always mutually exclusive. Moreover, the impulses Shakespeare gives to the Cade mob are hardly integral to the play; they do not provide obvious balance, contrast, or necessary conflict.

Unlike the examples of source conversion just drawn from *Richard II* and *Romeo and Juliet,* the alterations found in *Coriolanus* can be explained in dramatic terms. It is clearly Shakespeare's intention in this play to give us a protagonist who outdoes himself in crusty behavior which flouts every sensible recommendation made by his advisers. Like Richard II, Coriolanus is egocentrically incapable of using political reality as a frame of action, and he belongs, moreover, with Lear and Timon as a dedicated servant of unreason, a monument to the tradition of humor and crotchet characters. Shakespeare here simply dramatizes Plutarch's prescription:

For this Martius' natural wit and great heart did marvelously stir up his courage to do and attempt notable acts. But on the other side, for lack of education, he was so choleric and impatient, that he would yield to no living creature: which made him churlish, uncivil, and altogether unfit for any man's conversation. Yet men marvelling much at his constancy . . . thereupon they well liked his stoutness and temperancy. But for all that, they could not be acquainted with him . . . his behaviour was so unpleasant to them by reason of a certain insolent and stern manner he had.[48]

When Shakespeare began *Coriolanus,* he was confronted by source material which had thus pre-established the central character. Lacking, however, among the factors desirable in a play were contrast and balanced opposition. For if folly was to be balanced by folly, and a hero drawn who was not merely self-subsisting in his tragic flaws, what more likely device than to have altered the source so that the citizenry and tribunes exhibit faults which balance those of Corio-

[48] *Ibid.,* p. 138.

lanus? A play requires action and counter-action, temperament and counter-temperament, and to infer solely from Shakespeare's addition of these things that he was preoccupied with political emphasis against the citizenry would be a little like inferring from his portrait of Lady Macbeth, likewise designed for supplemental contrast, that he intended a doctrinaire attack upon women. Once we grant, moreover, that Shakespeare sought in *Coriolanus* a parallel balancing of factions more telling than the one his source gave him, we then encounter the truism that folly of the citizenry, when exhibited by dramatic means, will become much more vivid than it would be in a simple nondramatic narrative. The dramatic form alone accounts for part of the increased emphasis.

At this stage of discussion one might conclude that we are on our way to traditional dismissal of the problem, to that venerable platitude about Shakespeare being an artist who never—well, hardly ever—intended his plays to carry heavy doctrinal freight. On the contrary, the conclusion reached at this point is merely that play-source comparisons, particularly in the case of *Coriolanus,* are not good indications of a dramatist's political emphasis if the apparent increase or change of stress can be explained upon dramatic grounds. The problem of the next section will be to find criteria more serviceable than those of source study for the determination of ethical emphasis in drama.

DRAMATIC EMPHASIS OF IDEAS

Contrary to belief in some quarters, playwrights are often interested in ideas, which is not to say that they are uninterested in entertainment. No one conversant with plays will deny the entertainment value of thought presented in terms of concrete artistry, and it is largely this factor of entertainment value which has led to development in dramatic art of devices for transmitting doctrine to audiences. It is possible, moreover, to infer from a dramatist's use of these devices the ideas which he intends to impress upon his hearers and readers. In the analysis to follow but one assumption is required, the modest one that a practiced dramatist intends the normal responses of an audience to certain didactic and climactic methods of presentation. Some of these are significant enough to call for general discussion.

Accentuation of an idea in early exposition.—In *Hamlet* the careful foundation laid even for collateral ideas is shown by the ghost's emphatic disclosure that he was murdered before he had been confessed and absolved, "cut off even in the blossoms of my sin . . . O, horrible! O, horrible! most horrible." Doctrinal preparation is thus made for the telling anticlimax of the play in which Hamlet will not kill the praying king, but will wait till he is "in th' incestuous pleasure of his bed . . . or about some act that has no relish of salvation in 't." Another and more important belief upon which the play depends is the conception the audience must entertain that a ghost has power to assume forms and may be the devil or other evil spirit who has come to deceive and damn rather than to incite a just revenge. If this key idea is missed, the central device of the play within the play, and, consequently, the play itself throughout Act II and well into Act III, either become nonsense or require as explanation one of the theories of Hamlet's pale rationalization. It is not Shakespeare's fault, however, that later interpreters have ignored his skilled emphasis of the issue in early exposition. Hamlet's clear response upon being told of the ghost is, "If it assume my noble father's person, I'll speak to it though hell itself should gape." In Scene 4 his first words as he confronts the apparition are:

> Be thou a spirit of health or goblin damn'd,
> Bring with thee airs from heaven or blasts from hell,
> Be thy intents wicked or charitable,

Thou com'st in such a questionable shape
That I will speak to thee.

Later in the same scene, as Hamlet is about to follow the
beckoning spirit, Horatio interposes.

What if it tempt you toward the flood, my lord,
Or to the dreadful summit of the cliff
That beetles o'er his base into the sea,
And there assume some other horrible form. . . ?

Finally, in Scene 5, Hamlet again speaks to the point, this
time not with doubt or conjecture, but with belief: "Touching this vision here, it is an honest ghost, that let me tell you."
Hamlet is momentarily convinced that the ghost is not fraud-
ulent, but the audience has gone through impressive initia-
tion into the idea that the ghost's veracity is in issue, that it is
a being empowered to assume various forms, and that these
forms, as well as the message the ghost brings, may be either
spurious or genuine. There is accordingly no ground for
surprise later, when Hamlet, planning the play, observes
that the spirit he has seen may be the devil, or when, at the
climactic moment the mousetrap is sprung, he exclaims to
Horatio that he now will "take the ghost's word for a thousand pound." Initial exposition staged repetitively at key
points of the first act has prepared the way.

This discussion of *Hamlet,* perhaps elementary, is inserted
only to show how careful Shakespeare can be to equip an
audience with a governing idea at the beginning of a play.
Other examples are readily available: initial establishment of
the theme of hesitation and sensitivity to guilt in *Macbeth,*
of the shakiness of a crown won by usurpation in *Henry IV,*
of the virus of civil strife in *Romeo and Juliet,* of disunity in
Troilus and Cressida. This is not to say that Shakespeare
makes wholesale disclosure in preliminary exposition. From
the examples given, however, it is safe to conclude that when
expositional emphasis of an idea has actually appeared, it is

bad practice to ignore it or discount it as a clue to the dramatist's intentions.

Application of this principle to plays which deal with the populace should prove interesting. The Cade scenes form an isolated episode in a loose chronicle play and for that reason are not anticipated by audience orientation, but *Coriolanus* contains quick and sure initial emphasis, Scene 1 presenting a company of mutinous citizens armed with staves, clubs, and other weapons. They exchange angry manifestoes about the surfeiting rich, whose excess alone might relieve the public want were the rich decent enough to share it. Some wish to kill Caius Marcius; others are not so inclined; and while their parley continues, word comes that "the other side o' th' city is risen." The shout goes up, "Why stay we prating here?" At this moment Menenius enters and, as the shouting recedes, exorcises the multitude with his fable of the belly and the members. The conservative, doctrinaire content of this fable and the application of it have already been described; the pertinent factor here is that the fable and the disorder which precedes it provide the first impression made upon an audience.

Julius Caesar affords an even more elaborate example of expositional emphasis. As in *Coriolanus,* Scene 1 presents a spectacle of public gathering and threatened disorder. Here the first words of the play come from Flavius the tribune, who with great spleen orders home the idle mechanics infesting the public square. After some bickering and comedy it appears that the artisans have assembled to rejoice in Caesar's triumph, and at this early point Marullus attacks the citizens for a collective trait which, following Antony's oration, is to provide the turning point of the play. This trait, wavering political allegiance, is dramatized without delay; the citizens are accused of forgetting Pompey in their favoring of Caesar; they are called blocks, stones, "worse than senseless things," who have climbed walls, battlements, and even chimney tops to see Pompey in the streets of Rome, while now they make uproarious assemblage to greet today's hero who "comes in triumph over Pompey's blood." Thus, in the beginning sixty lines of *Julius Caesar* there is established the inconstancy which will lead the populace to smile upon Brutus and immediately thereafter upon Antony. Scene 2 then consolidates this initial conception with accounts by Casca of the unstable multitude tossing their caps into the air as Caesar refuses the crown.

Finally, at the conclusion of Scene 3 the conspirator Cinna is presented to the audience with noticeable care. Although not an important character, he comes onstage prominently and is singled out by name four times within ten lines as he is dispatched with a message to Brutus. Cinna, it will be remembered, is the conspirator whom the mob of Act III will imagine it is about to assault and murder as it lays hands upon another Cinna, the poet, who is on his way to Caesar's funeral. That Shakespeare intended this mob scene to be significant beyond the mere providing of melodramatic relief is made probable by the care taken in early exposition to identify Cinna the conspirator, so that later the grisly irony of the mob's mistake will be quite clear to the audience.

The principle that a skilled dramatist should be taken seriously in his communication of first impressions is emphasized by the peculiar nature of a dramatist's task in preliminary exposition. There is no stage in the writing of a play at which less concession can be made to nonessentials; the multiple responsibility of introducing characters, of establishing the framework of fact and mood, and of simultaneously putting the story into forward momentum is one which makes exceptional demands of economy and clarity. An experienced craftsman at this stage of composition tends strictly to business and is unlikely to include, even accidentally, material which is not significant.

Use of choral characters.—This second method of doctrinal emphasis is well understood by most readers of Shakespeare; as a device it requires no description, but the technique of its use in political plays and scenes needs comment. The dramatic timing of choral material is the factor which is impressive. The Bishop of Carlisle's denunciation of usurpers occurs unemphatically in Holinshed at a time later than Bolingbroke's assumption of the kingship. In the play, however, Bolingbroke, who has been informed by York of "plume-pluck'd" Richard's abdication, exclaims, "In God's name I'll ascend the regal throne," and at this climactic moment Shakespeare's Carlisle breaks in with his diatribe and prophecy which provides chorally the political idea around which the entire Shakespearean chronicle history cycle is written.

Another choral character is Escalus, Prince of Verona in *Romeo and Juliet.* His rhetorical dressing down of the perpetrators of civil strife is commonly known but, again, it is well to observe how Shakespeare has timed its occurrence: it comes after the brawl of the first scene has reached a peak by infiltration of one group of combatants after another, capped by the entry of old Montague and old Capulet. The Prince strides onstage and, as the fracas subsides to a murmur, rebukes the brawlers with a veritable Tudor curse upon profaners of the public peace. Shakespeare uses the same method of emphasis in *Julius Caesar* and *Coriolanus.* It has already been observed that both of these plays open with scenes of public disorder, but it remains to be noted of both of them that commentary upon the disorder is timed for the silence which follows assumption of authority by the choral character. Marullus, in *Julius Caesar,* with his denunciatory speech on the crowd's fickleness, and Menenius, in *Coriolanus,* with his fable of the belly and the members, both proclaim political morality to the audience at this highly strategic point.

The remaining choral character is Alexander Iden, esquire,

of Kent, who kills Jack Cade and hallows his sword with a declamatory speech. His commentary upon the significance of his act has already been quoted, and it is only necessary to indicate Shakespeare's forceful staging of it. Iden, it will be recalled, has been meditating upon the modest luxury of country retirement when he encounters in his garden the wan fugitive who forces an unequal fight. The chivalrous Iden reluctantly wounds the rebel, and only when the latter is dying does he discover whom he has struck down. The result is a moral paroxysm, through which the audience not only hears choral commentary upon the killing of Cade, but hears it from a gentle character dramatically transformed into an executioner. Emphasis upon the deed's significance is thus doubled, and it may be remembered that Shakespeare substituted Hall's version for Holinshed's in order to achieve this.

Emphasis of doctrine by the "tables turned" device.—Students of Shakespeare are aware of the fallacy of subjective interpretation; the various correctives which barricade the way against seekers after Shakespeare's meaning have been reared so high that enigma is looked upon as a special possession of the dramatist and has gradually come to be celebrated for its own sake. It is time, however, that this devotion to skepticism be tempered with a realization, objective as any, that there are certain ways of telling a story which are so sure to leave their mark upon an audience that any trained dramatist who employs them can be held accountable for the result. The turn of events in Act IV, Scene 1, of *The Merchant of Venice* could have but one foreseen effect upon an audience which has watched Shylock prepare his luckless trap for Antonio. Here the tables are abruptly turned, and the very conditions of the bond are used against its contriver. Even an unadorned employment of the device would score heavily against Shylock, but Shakespeare goes much further. Shylock has gloated, "A Daniel come to judgment! yea, a second

Daniel!" and as Portia decrees that Antonio prepare his breast for the knife, he has exclaimed, "O noble judge!" Then as her decision is made more explicit, he echoes himself, "Most rightful judge!" and three lines later cries, "Most learned judge!" Immediately, however, the qualification about shedding blood is added to Portia's decree, and it is now Gratiano's turn: "O upright judge! Mark, Jew: O learned judge!" Four lines later he shouts, "O learned judge! Mark, Jew: a learned judge!" and five lines after that, "O Jew! an upright judge, a learned judge!" Finally, as the judgment is completed, Gratiano's mockery reverts to Shylock's original self-congratulatory line as Gratiano crows, "A second Daniel! A Daniel, Jew!" to which he shortly adds, "A Daniel, still say I, a second Daniel! I thank thee, Jew, for teaching me that word."

There is fairly general agreement that interpretation of *The Merchant of Venice* which ignores or runs counter to this forceful repudiation of Shylock gains through wishfulness only what it loses by total irresponsibility. It is not generally agreed, however, that Shakespeare intends to cast the main onus of villainy upon the tribunes and the citizenry in *Coriolanus*. Yet, at a position in this play [49] directly analogous to that of the trial scene in *The Merchant of Venice,* occurs the same heavily ironic reversal and the same repetitive commentary upon its meaning, which is that the populace is responsible for Rome's disaster. As the truth of Coriolanus' alliance with the Volscians penetrates the wits of the tribunes, Cominius enters with the comment upon them, "O, you have made good work!" When the news becomes clear to Menenius, he echoes Cominius, "You have made fair work, I fear me." His contempt increases as the tribunes become helplessly discomfited, and he flouts them again, "You have made good work, you and your apron men." And some twenty lines later there is the cry,

[49] Act IV, scene 6.

You have made fair hands,
You and your crafts! You have crafted fair!

The citizens enter and, in keeping with their stereotyped fickleness, protest individually that they had been opposed to the banishment of Coriolanus all the while, to which Menenius repeats his choral taunt, "You have made good work, you and your cry!" And as though the repeated emphasis had not been sufficient, Menenius two scenes later rebukes the tribunes again.

Why, so; you have made good work!
A pair of tribunes that have rack'd for Rome
To make coals cheap! A noble memory!

The tables have been turned upon "representative democracy," and the audience is hardly allowed to forget it.

Emphasis by gratuitous distortion.—It has been previously conceded that a playwright's point of view cannot be inferred from distortion of source material, if the distortion can be laid to dramatic expediency or to simple vitality of the dramatic medium. Ordinary dramatic distortion presents even greater difficulties of interpretation, for it is likely to appear in plays merely through imitation and to be innocuous to audiences because of long usage. We are confronted here with the elementary fact that commoners and mechanics were stock butts of comedy on the Elizabethan stage, and were often so used to their very faces in the pit. Such a convention is not without significance, for it is obviously an important clue to the times, just as employment of the negro as a comic butt is an important and depressing sign of our times. But it is impossible to be sure from this standard form of distortion that a dramatist, taken individually, is using it for ideological purposes, or that his audience is even conscious of it.

There is a great difference, however, between conventional distortion and gratuitous distortion, which either may go beyond customary practice or may not be conventional at all. In dramatizing the populace Shakespeare offers a remarkable example of this by emphasis upon crowd stench to such an extent that inconstancy, the mob's conventional attribute, is sometimes forced into the background. Georg Brandes considered this a reflection of Shakespeare's personal contempt for part of his audience, and because Brandes' opinion must be reviewed thoroughly on other grounds, the discussion which would normally follow here will appear in the third chapter. When consideration of the theme is there resumed, it will be found gratuitous and therefore an effective indication of didactic intention.

The foregoing analysis of three plays and of certain Shakespearean methods of emphasis has been designed to arouse the fresh curiosity necessary for attacking old problems. It would be easy at this point to move directly into a survey of criticism and interpretation of the antidemocratic elements in Shakespeare which have been reviewed, but fairness calls for a brief postponement of this. Untouched thus far has been another side of Shakespeare which ought to be examined.

A DELIBERATE AND PLEASANT DIGRESSION

Conventional aristocratic attitudes of tolerance for isolated unfortunates are not related to the issue of democracy, especially when combined with a stern sense of social hierarchy. It is true, of course, that sympathizers with democracy exhibit these benevolent attitudes, but so did occasional feudal barons, Elizabethan landowners, or slaveholders of the eighteenth and nineteenth centuries. In reviewing the Cade scenes, *Julius Caesar,* and *Coriolanus,* there has been concern only for Shakespeare's portrait of commoners as a mass. And it should be apparent from the lack of any attempt to soften the picture he gives us that the purpose of this book is not to hint at political liberalism on Shakespeare's part where the total dramatic emphasis is incompatible with it.

Such unsentimental and logically restrictive treatment can lead, however, to serious misunderstanding, as well as to unwarranted bolstering of the "historical" attitude that Shakespeare was but Elizabethan in expressing contempt for oppressed majorities or minorities. If because it is technically irrelevant to do otherwise we allow Shakespeare to speak solely of political masses, he will be left undifferentiated from those of his time who were contemptuous not only of the common mass but of the comman man. To describe his tolerance of humble individuals may bear little relation to the problem raised by plays which satirize groups, but it will at least separate Shakespeare from those who also wrote drama like the Cade scenes but little or nothing to compensate for it. Similarly, to call attention to lines in *The Merchant of Venice* which are socially humane may be irrelevant to the total quality of that play as a pretty piece of Jew-baiting, but it will differentiate Shakespeare from theater spectators who applauded the Jew-baiting and missed the modicum of humanity.

Quite apart from his perversity in attacking the mass and quite apart from the patronizing which often accompanies defense of the lowly, there is nevertheless great charity in Shakespeare for the humble and the oppressed, as well as hatred for snobs of all varieties. Although it is aristocratic to the bone, insufferably so by modern standards, the speech of Theseus,[50] in graciously accepting the lamentable efforts of Bottom and company, ends with the lines,

> Love, therefore, and tongue-ti'd simplicity
> In least speak most.

And, while the Archbishop of Canterbury in *Henry V* is far less concerned for the poor than he is for loss of church lands, he is led to speak of

[50] *MND*, Act V, scene 1, ll. 89–105.

relief of lazars and weak age,
Of indigent faint souls past corporal toil.[51]

The significant element here is not the situation or the context or anything but the fact that Shakespeare could write such a passage on the wholly incidental theme of helplessness and poverty-ridden old age. Nor where humanity rather than political justice is the issue, does it matter whether King Henry replies to some free-thinking soldiers with that meretricious analogy about a father who sends his son on a venture which miscarries. What does matter is the feeling put into a speech of one of the soldiers; phrasing is a test of feeling, and there has seldom been such phrasing as this.

But if the cause be not good, the King himself hath a heavy reckoning to make, when all those legs and arms and heads, chopped off in a battle, shall join together at the latter day and cry all, "We died at such a place"; some swearing, some crying for a surgeon, some upon their wives left poor behind them, some upon the debts they owe, some upon their children rawly left. I am afeard there are few die well that die in a battle; for how can they charitably dispose of anything, when blood is their argument? Now if these men do not die well, it will be a black matter for the King that led them to it: who to disobey were against all proportion of subjection.[52]

One is well aware that Shakespeare probably considered this speech to be logically less convincing than Henry's reply to it. But if humanity is the capacity to entertain, not only intellectually but also emotionally, the views of less fortunate men, we have it here in generous measure. Shakespeare is not, however, the consistent humanitarian on this score; that much will have to be conceded, for the playwright who could assign such lines to a common soldier could also attempt to bring down the house, and probably succeed, with the spectacle of Falstaff's press gang in operation for recruitment to the King's forces.

[51] *Henry V*, Act I, scene 1, ll. 15–16.
[52] *Ibid.*, Act IV, scene 1, ll. 140–153.

Consistently or inconsistently, the humane point of view nevertheless recurs, and into its expression is packed all of Shakespeare's virtuosity.

> Poor naked wretches, wheresoe'er you are,
> That bide the pelting of this pitiless storm,
> How shall your houseless heads and unfed sides,
> Your loop'd and window'd raggedness, defend you
> From seasons such as these? [53]

These are words of the half-mad Lear. The character who speaks them and the playwright who wrote them may have been voicing utterly traditional sentiments, but no merely frigid traditionalist could have provided the passage with such phrasing.

In addition to his expression of pity for the weak, the poor, and the old, Shakespeare exhibits a trait so well known that no quoted examples of it are needed. This is a quality he shares with almost all dramatists of his day, a tendency to use the lowly as a medium for whimsical, pertinent, and often intelligent commentary. We need only recall Juliet's nurse, the soldiers in *Henry V*, or old Adam in *As You Like It*. And occasionally, as in *Lear*, this commentary assumes the dignity of a chorus. Even those despised characters, the citizens in *Coriolanus*, have their moments; there is a passage which warrants their intelligence, unusual forbearance, and sense of fair play under insupportable insult from Caius Marcius. At the awaited moment when the hero appears before the plebs in his gown of humility, the Third Citizen spotlights the strange sight.

Here he comes, and in the gown of humility; mark his behaviour. We are not to stay all together, but to come by him where he stands, by ones, by twos, and by threes. He's to make his requests by particulars, wherein every one of us has a single honour, in giving him our own voices with our own tongues; therefore follow me, and I'll direct you how you shall go by him.[54]

[53] *Lear,* Act III, scene 4, ll. 28–32.   [54] *Coriol.,* Act II, scene 3, ll. 44–52.

Then occurs a very odd scene, the arranged interview between Coriolanus and his plebeian electorate, and who shall say that the citizens fail us here?

> *Cor.* Pray you now, if it may stand with the tune of your voices that I may be consul, I have here the customary gown.
> *Fourth Cit.* You have deserved nobly of your country, and you have not deserved nobly.
> *Cor.* Your enigma?
> *Fourth Cit.* You have been a scourge to her enemies, you have been a rod to her friends; you have not indeed loved the common people.
> *Cor.* You should account me the more virtuous that I have not been common in my love. I will, sir, flatter my sworn brother, the people, to earn a dearer estimation of them; 'tis a condition they account gentle: and since the wisdom of their choice is rather to have my hat than my heart, I will practise the insinuating nod and be off to them most counterfeitly; that is, sir, I will counterfeit the bewitchment of some popular man and give it bountiful to the desirers. Therefore, beseech you, I may be consul.
> *Fifth Cit.* We hope to find you our friend; and therefore give you our voices heartily.
> *Fourth Cit.* You have received many wounds for your country.
> *Cor.* I will not seal your knowledge with showing them. I will make much of your voices, and so trouble you no further.
> *Both Cit.* The gods give you joy, sir, heartily! [55]

Frankness, tolerance, good manners, and plain dignity—these are qualities which Shakespeare not only grants to the citizens but also places in deliberate contrast with the miserable contempt which Coriolanus vents after they have gone.

So here is the issue as before. In the ultimate and conclusive emphasis which Shakespeare gives to the play, the citizens are repaid in ignominy for their presumptuous meddling in civic affairs; that is the political side of the question and the one with which we shall be concerned; but on the human side, which is another matter, Shakespeare has shown here that there is little in his portrait of lowly people which is coldly stacked against them.

Closely related in dramatic method to this aspect of *Corio-*

[55] *Ibid.,* ll. 91–118.

lanus is the presentation of Shylock. He is one of a persecuted minority who, when the total play is considered, emerges undone, mocked, and ridiculous. As for the play as a whole, we may applaud Hazelton Spencer's honest assertion: "I do not see how a Jew can read *The Merchant of Venice* without pain and indignation." [56] The point to be made, however, is that nowhere appears such scorn for thoughtless persecution as we hear in "Hath not a Jew eyes?" and the words which follow; that seldom has a prig been confronted with anything like the familiar lines:

> Go to, then! You come to me, and you say,
> "Shylock, we would have moneys"; you say so—
> You, that did void your rheum upon my beard
> And foot me as you spurn a stranger cur
> Over your threshold; moneys is your suit.
> What should I say to you? Should I not say,
> "Hath a dog money? Is it possible
> A cur can lend three thousand ducats?" Or
> Shall I bend low and in a bondman's key,
> With bated breath and whisp'ring humbleness,
> Say this:
> "Fair sir, you spat on me on Wednesday last;
> You spurn'd me such a day; another time
> You call'd me dog; and for these courtesies
> I'll lend you thus much moneys?" [57]

But in Shakespeare's eyes Antonio was not a prig, and the lines quoted were meant to be ridiculous in their defensive overstatement. Thus runs a familiar refrain. Perhaps so; the arguments for such interpretation are well enough understood. But there is a point at which intuition becomes so strong that it controls; the critics of this school have yet to demonstrate that Shakespeare invariably yielded to stereotypes or that he could not momentarily rise beyond the character, the play, and the age. If he ever did, it was here. Nor have they disposed of the possibility of ambivalence, and Shake-

[56] *The Art and Life of William Shakespeare*, p. 240.
[57] *MV*, Act I, scene 3, ll. 116–130.

speare's ambivalence is at the root of the current discussion.
Shakespeare's obvious scorn for snobs is the next humaniz-
ing trait which calls for attention. Simple mention of characters like Osric, Malvolio, and the Dauphin in *Henry V* will
exemplify it, but there is one episode which is singular: in
extenuation of the rebuff which he gave to the king's messenger, Hotspur describes a "certain lord" who caused him to
forget all courtesy, the nobleman who appeared late upon
the battlefield with the air of a bridegroom, smelling like a
milliner, and with skin "new-reaped [which] show'd like a
stubble-land at harvest home." This is the precious baron
who talks "like a waiting-gentlewoman of guns and drums
and wounds,—God save the mark!" It is the "popinjay"
who remarks that gunpowder has taken the manly romance
out of war. In the next chapter notice must be taken of Shakespeare's preoccupation with the stench of massed commoners.
In Hotspur's speech about the popinjay, however, are lines
which show this tendency not to have been altogether one-
sided.

> And 'twixt his finger and his thumb he held
> A pouncet box, which ever and anon
> He gave his nose and took 't away again;
> Who therewith angry, when it next came there,
> Took it in snuff; and still he smil'd and talk'd,
> And as the soldiers bore dead bodies by,
> He call'd them untaught knaves, unmannerly,
> To bring a slovenly unhandsome corse
> Betwixt the wind and his nobility.[58]

Although Shakespeare was content to depict consistent disgust on the part of aristocrats for the smell of the lowly, he
still could offer a situation like this in which aristocratic nos-
trils quiver in contemptible fashion. And although this episode in no way softens or explains away his general practice,
it does enlarge our conception of the dramatist who could
offer it so eloquently.

[58] *I Henry IV*, Act I, scene 3, ll. 36–45.

Nor in an effort to understand Shakespeare fully should we forget what traditional critics have always emphasized: that while he may exhibit the populace as politically imbecile, he grants them no exclusive possession of governmental stupidity or depravity. Professors Thaler and Falk have shown that while Walt Whitman began with hostility toward Shakespeare for expressing decayed feudal ideals, he later modified his view with the interesting thesis that Shakespeare dramatized the corruption and incompetence of feudal maladministration.[59] From a certain standpoint this is true. The dethronement of Richard II, although it leads inevitably in Shakespeare to civil war, was nevertheless in his view the dethronement of a regal sentimentalist whose incompetency was insupportable; and while future ages groaned for the act of usurpation, they groaned only because rival gangs of the corrupt elite fought each other to exhaustion. The difficulty one has with traditional interpreters of the populace in Shakespeare arises, not from their demonstration that his aristocrats are also often murderers or bunglers, but from their inference that since the attribution of evil to the populace is balanced by the attribution of evil to other classes, it is therefore in little need of attention or explanation.

A final qualification of Shakespeare's social point of view is suggested by an episode in *The Tempest*. Alonso, Sebastian, Antonio, and Gonzalo find themselves idle and at cross purposes following the shipwreck. In the course of that drifting, irrelevant, and at times irritable talk which is the diversion of soldiers in a replacement area, of sailors off watch at sea, or of men in a strange land with nothing to do, conversation not unnaturally gets round to the problem of remaking human institutions. Especially is this true when there is an oldster present who has reinforced his ideas with some random reading. Such a one is Gonzalo; he has been worked over and verbally kicked about by the others, but with that uncon-

[59] See notes 24 and 25, Chapter III.

cern of men without ego he rises to the bait once more. Do
the others know what he would do had he "the plantation of
this isle?" Do they know what he would do were he the king
of it? "He'd sow it with nettle-seed," observes Antonio, who
can be imagined chewing a spear of grass. No, honestly, what
do they really think he'd do?

Gon. I' th' commonwealth I would by contraries
　Execute all things; for no kind of traffic
　Would I admit; no name of magistrate;
　Letters should not be known; riches, poverty,
　And use of service, none; contract, succession,
　Bourn, bound of land, tilth, vineyard, none;
　No use of metal, corn, or wine, or oil;
　No occupation; all men idle, all;
　And women too, but innocent and pure;
　No sovereignty;—
Seb. 　　　　　　Yet he would be king on't.
Ant. The latter end of his commonwealth forgets the beginning.
Gon. All things in common nature should produce
　Without sweat or endeavour: treason, felony,
　Sword, pike, knife, gun, or need of any engine,
　Would I not have; but nature should bring forth,
　Of it own kind, all foison, all abundance,
　To feed my innocent people.
Seb. No marrying 'mong his subjects?
Ant. None, man; all idle; whores and knaves.
Gon. I would with such perfection govern, sir,
　T'excel the golden age.
Seb. 　　　　　　Save his Majesty!
Ant. Long live Gonzalo!
Gon. 　　　　　And,—do you mark me, sir?
Alon. Prithee, no more; thou dost talk nothing to me.
Gon. I do well believe your Highness; and did it to minister occasion
　to these gentlemen, who are of such sensible and nimble lungs that
　they always use to laugh at nothing.
Ant. 'Twas you we laughed at.
Gon. Who in this kind of merry fooling am nothing to you; so you may
　continue and laugh at nothing still.
Ant. What a blow was there given!
Seb. An it had not fallen flatlong.

Gon. You are gentlemen of brave mettles; you would lift the moon
out of her sphere, if she would continue in it five weeks without
changing.[60]

The situation here is remarkable in its disposition of those
who try to analyze, classify, and make summation of Shakespeare's attitudes. For one thing, Gonzalo's ideal of the good
society is rich in the tradition exemplified by More's *Utopia;*
for another it stems immediately from Shakespeare's reading
of Montaigne. On the other hand, to many people of Shakespeare's day it must have expressed doctrine similar to the
leveling program, notoriously "Antibaptistical," which was
a favorite object of attack by those opposed to religious dissent.[61] To complicate the question further, Gonzalo is not
too serious and is obviously a little weak in the facts-of-life
department; nor is he too gifted with consistency, as the
"realists" in the party are delighted to point out. But who are
these realists? No better certified materialists or opportun-
ists could be recruited from Shakespeare's plays than they.
And who, after all, is Gonzalo but the stanch, loyal, and un-
corrupted follower addressed by Prospero toward the end of
the play as "good Gonzalo, my true preserver"? Add that
The Tempest was written toward the last, that it conveys
the quiet of evening, and the equalitarian notions of Gonzalo
are a little hard to place as something the dramatist drew
from Montaigne for comic relief only. Do they imply that
the author of *Coriolanus* had softened? Experienced people
know that golden-age sentimentalism is conventional, that it
often accompanies the most resolute political conservatism,
and that there is nothing fundamentally democratic about
it. So the less speculation on that score, the better. Gonzalo's
ideas have nothing really to do with the tribunes, with the
Roman plebeians, or with Jack Cade, but they do help to fore-
stall an arbitrary judgment of Shakespeare.

[60] *Tempest,* Act II, scene 1, ll. 147–184. [61] See Chapter IV.

CHAPTER III

Types of Interpretation

A READER of Shakespeare's plays about the populace will not be surprised that in the nineteenth century there were interesting attempts to interpret this dramatic material and that in our own time increasing attention has been given to it. During the recent past there has been such concern over social and political democracy and, simu! sn-eously, such a growth of Shakespeare scholarship that a merging of the two currents has been inevitable. The purpose of this book, however, is not to offer a history of the issue, but rather to meet it; and while a review of interpretation is necessary, neither a bibliographical nor a chronological survey of previous work will lead logically to the problem. For present needs it will be better to group interpreters according to types and to exemplify each of these so that every major trend of scholarship will be examined and the important differences of opinion defined.

The significant classes of investigation can be understood best if discussion begins with the biographical critics, whose emphasis has been upon personal reasons Shakespeare may have had for presentation of his mob scenes. Following this, survey may be made of the attack upon Shakespeare by those who have taken exception to his handling of the populace. Next reviewed will be Marxist interpreters, who have evinced a special defense against that attack, and finally will appear an account of traditional or orthodox criticism which has also risen to Shakespeare's defense in several characteristic ways.

The method in general will be to attempt evaluation of these
divergent points of view as each is described.

BIOGRAPHICAL INTERPRETATION

The inevitable attempt has been made to find reflection of
Shakespeare's personal sensitivity in his depiction of the
multitude, and this has been part of the general effort, traditionally discredited, to discover the attitudes of Shakespeare
in the plays. Attention centers immediately upon Georg
Brandes who, writing of *Coriolanus* and of Shakespeare's
"hatred of the masses," asserts that the dramatist's social
point of view "is as personal as it well could be." Shakespeare's dislike of the mob "was based upon his contempt for
their discrimination, but it had its deepest roots in the purely
physical repugnance of his artist nerves to their plebeian atmosphere." Later, after agreeing that *Coriolanus* reflects
contemporary politics, Brandes nevertheless adds that "the
antidemocratic spirit and passion of the play sprang from no
momentary political situation, but from Shakespeare's heart
of hearts," and he finds this revulsion evolving from the
faltering efforts of Shakespeare's youth on to the period of
Coriolanus. Brandes is now even more specific, as he supplies
a motive for this loathing: as for the populace, "it was in
plain words their evil smell which repelled Shakespeare. He
was the true artist in this respect too, and more sensitive
to noxious fumes than any woman." Then, alluding to the
term "stinkards," which was applied to occupants of the
pit, Brandes decides that penny spectators at the theater
were prime factors in Shakespeare's contempt for the
masses.[1]

Whatever may be said of Brandes' intuition, it can be
granted that he does not employ it to find in Shakespeare a
democratic tolerance; in fact he attacks several interpreters,

---

[1] The statements and quotations from Brandes are from *William Shakespeare* (English translation, New York, The Macmillan Company, 1935),
pp. 532–550.

notably Hudson, who have followed this equally intuitive
course, and is one of the few critics who have made no attempt
to attenuate or explain away the issue. The part of his approach which calls for critical analysis, however, is not his
unsentimental realism; it is his ascription to Shakespeare of
the personal motives which have been described. It is clear,
of course, to every modern student of Shakespeare that the
practice of reading the plays as autobiographical documents
is initially suspect, and indeed many would reject this pro-
cedure as romantic criticism on its most callow level. The
writer, for one, at a preliminary stage of investigation did
so without hesitation, but a growing conviction that "objective" interpretation of Shakespeare has hardened into
dogma led to examination and enlargement of Brandes' evidence and finally to the decision that his claims should be
reconsidered.

As the facts are assembled, it is uncomfortably apparent
that when Shakespeare's commoners gather, something occurs which with slight whimsicality could be called a collective
halitosis of democracy in action. Anyone who has read in
sequence the Cade scenes, *Julius Caesar,* and *Coriolanus* may
have been uneasy at the motif of proletarian stench which
occurs in all three plays, and in *Coriolanus* becomes a minor
obsession. This has been noticed by many, but Brandes happens to be the only interpreter who has described it with any
particularity. An offering of details may strike the average
reader as literary garbage-picking, but, if so, he is advised
to read *Coriolanus* through at a sitting, to compare it with
certain non-Shakespearean plays and scenes,[2] and to decide
for himself whether the subject, however unpleasant, looms
large enough in Shakespeare to merit discussion. In the end,
at least one conclusion may be prominent: a conviction that
the association in Shakespeare of stench with *demos* is hardly
explainable as a mere dramatic device (unless every emphasis

[2] A number of these are discussed in Chapter V.

by a dramatist be considered purely dramatic) or as a practice common in Elizabethan literature. Whatever personal
impulses may have evoked this from Shakespeare, it falls
clearly into the category of gratuitous accentuation which
as biographical data cannot be glibly dismissed.

As a proposal is made that the laws of England henceforth
issue from Jack Cade's mouth, one of his henchmen remarks,
"Nay, John, it will be stinking law; for his breath stinks with
eating toasted cheese." [3] When Casca describes the scene of
Caesar's refusal of the crown, he tells Brutus and Cassius
that the citizens "threw up their sweaty night-caps and
uttered such a deal of stinking breath" that Caesar fainted,
while he, Casca, dared not laugh for fear of breathing the
bad air.[4]

These unaffectionate attributions of evil smell to the populace are well known, of course, and would be insignificant by
themselves. They are preludes, however, to a later and almost abandoned use of the notion in *Coriolanus*. In the opening scene one of the citizenry, though defiant, is a little rueful
about the common affliction: "They say poor suitors have
strong breaths; they shall know we have strong arms too." [5]
In Act II one of the tribunes reports that he has heard Coriolanus swear that he would never show his wounds to the
people to "beg their stinking breaths," and Coriolanus, when
urged by Menenius to speak with the citizens, tells him: "Bid
them wash their faces and keep their teeth clean." [6] Coriolanus speaks of the "mutable, rank-scented many" in a subsequent scene,[7] and his later retort to the sentence of banishment is:

> You common cry of curs! whose breath I hate
> As reek o' th' rotten fens, whose loves I prize
> As the dead carcasses of unburied men
> That do corrupt my air, I banish you! [8]

[3] *2 Henry VI*, Act IV, scene 7, ll. 12–13.   [4] *JC*, Act I, scene 2, ll. 246–252.
[5] *Coriol.*, Act I, scene 1, ll. 60–62.   [6] *Ibid.*, Act II, scene 3, ll. 66–67.
[7] *Ibid.*, Act III, scene 1, l. 66.   [8] *Ibid.*, Act III, scene 3, ll. 120–123.

If this surging disgust with the people were confined to
Coriolanus himself it would be "in character" and perhaps
little else, for that redoubtable patrician is, to understate
the matter, both prejudiced and plain-spoken. Menenius,
however, described by a citizen as one who "hath loved the
common people," is no less forthright when he denounces
the tribunes' constituency as "the voice of occupation and the
breath of garlic eaters," [9] and soon afterward, in lines clearly
reminiscent of Casca in *Julius Caesar,* beards the citizens
themselves:

> You are they
> That made the air unwholesome when you cast
> Your stinking greasy caps in hooting at
> Coriolanus' exile.[10]

These two outbursts from Menenius are doubly meaningful
because they both occur at the height of a tables-turned scene,
the significance of which has been discussed in a previous
chapter.

As the play draws to a close, Menenius and Cominius strike
the note again, this time in final summation. Cominius has
appealed to Coriolanus to have consideration at least for
his friends, and he tells Menenius, within hearing of the
tribunes,

> His answer to me was,
> He could not stay to pick them in a pile
> Of noisome musty chaff. He said 'twas folly,
> For one poor grain or two, to leave unburnt
> And still to nose th' offence.[11]

Menenius echoes, "For one poor grain or two!" exclaims,
"We are the grains!" and declares of the tribunes,

> You are the musty chaff, and you are smelt
> Above the moon; we must be burnt for you.[12]

---

[9] *Ibid.,* Act IV, scene 6, ll. 95–98. [10] *Ibid.,* ll. 129–132.
[11] *Ibid.,* Act V, scene 1, ll. 24–28. [12] *Ibid.,* Act V, scene 1, ll. 31–32.

The language here is, perhaps, figurative, but the association of populace and stench remains unvarying to the end. The lines just quoted, moreover, occur in a repetition of the tables-turned episode of two scenes earlier. As though the first application had not been enough, here is the same formula, humiliation of the citizens by harping upon their evil smell, and the same refrain line, "You have made good work," to accompany the insult.

Shakespeare, unlike other dramatists of his time, seems to have been reminded automatically of olfactory dismay when writing of artisans as a group. Even the good-humored handling of Bottom's friends and their amateur theatricals finds the inevitable theme included: "And most dear actors, eat no onions or garlic, for we are to utter sweet breath." [13] Octavius Caesar, in reviewing Antony's unsubdued conduct in Egypt, grants tolerantly that it is not amiss

> To reel the streets at noon, and stand the buffet
> With knaves that smell of sweat.[14]

And as Cleopatra tries to imagine the worst of being taken captive to Rome, there is the venerable refrain:

> Mechanic slaves
> With greasy aprons, rules and hammers, shall
> Uplift us to the view; in their thick breaths,
> Rank of gross diet, shall we be enclouded,
> And forc'd to drink their vapor.[15]

The serpent of old Nile has studied easy ways to die. She is a connoisseur of ways to Nirvana, and swooning, as did Caesar, because of the breath of mechanics is apparently not one of them.

It is upon such evidence, although upon data not so complete, that Brandes rests his case. And corroborative to some extent of his belief that Shakespeare's disgust stemmed from personal contact with theater audiences, there are two inter-

---

[13] *MND,* Act IV, scene 2, ll. 43–44.   [14] *AC,* Act I, scene 4, ll. 20–21.
[15] *Ibid.,* Act V, scene 2, ll. 209–213.

esting bits of evidence which Brandes did not consider. Casca's lines about stinking breath are followed immediately
by:

> If the tag-rag people did not clap him and hiss him, according as he
> pleased and displeased them, as they use to do the players in the theater,
> I am no true man.[16]

Provocatively enough, reference to theaters closely follows
Cleopatra's speech, previously quoted, on the horrors of being delivered over to a smelly populace.

> The quick comedians
> Extemporally will stage us, and present
> Our Alexandrian revels; Antony
> Shall be brought drunken forth, and I shall see
> Some squeaking Cleopatra boy my greatness
> I' th' posture of a whore.[17]

That Shakespeare on two occasions completes passages on
crowd stench and commotion with satirical allusion to play-
houses is interesting as a sample of his free-association processes.

Several queries will have occurred to a critical reader of
this perhaps lamentable, perhaps amusing, but necessary discussion. Are the commoners in Shakespeare, after all, the
only social class to which he applies the attribute of offensive
smell? And even if they are, does the phenomenon amount
to a literary or dramatic convention? Answers to these questions reinforce conclusions already suggested.

So far as can be determined, there are but three possible
Shakespearean applications of this theme to characters other
than "mechanics" or artisans, and all of them are to be dis-
counted for various reasons. In Mercutio's speech there is
the well-known line about Mab plaguing the lips of ladies
with blisters, "because their breaths with sweetmeets tainted
are," [18] which is quite innocuous and good-humored. If the

[16] *JC*, Act I, scene 2, ll. 260-263. [17] *AC*, Act V, scene 2, ll. 216-221.
[18] *RJ*, Act I, scene 4, ll. 75-76.

Epilogue in *As You Like It* was intended for an aristocratic audience, Rosalind's words might have some bearing upon the subject, although they too have the light and incidental touch.

If I were a woman I would kiss as many of you as had beards that pleased me, complexions that liked me, and breaths that I defied not.

The remaining example is from *Cymbeline*. The First Lord says ironically,

Sir, I would advise you to shift a shirt; the violence of action hath made you reek as a sacrifice. Where air comes out, air comes in; there's none abroad so wholesome as that you vent.[19]

But this is limited by the interesting fact that it is Cloten, hardly an exemplar of *noblesse oblige,* who receives the advice. There is an obvious divergence of these passages from the norm of derision and contempt shown by those directed at the populace. If they demonstrate anything, it is that Shakespeare was perfectly conscious of living at a time when even the well-born were not devoted to bathing and oral hygiene and that the aversion certain of his characters exhibit toward commoners on that score is consequently the more arbitrary.

A critical reader will also wish to know whether Shakespeare's images or designations of olfactory disgust which refer to the populace are simply part of a general tendency on his part to overdo the theme of repellent smell. If so, the association of it with popular assemblage cannot be considered a special emphasis, although it still would remain quite relevant as an ascription of unpleasantness to the citizenry, and an inveterate one at that.

It is natural to turn here to Miss Spurgeon's study of Shakespeare's imagery.[20] She finds that Shakespeare is particularly sensitive to evil odors, but the two main categories of this which she lists are decaying corpses and the populace

---

[19] *Cymb.,* Act I, scene 2, ll. 1–5.

[20] Caroline Spurgeon, *Shakespeare's Imagery and What It Tells Us* (New York, The Macmillan Company, 1935), pp. 78–81.

itself, and since she does not begin to exhaust the references already reviewed, it must be assumed that her tabulations here are for exemplification only. If one wishes to take the trouble and does not mind feeling a little ridiculous, one may discover from the *Concordance* that Shakespeare's uses of the word "smell" and its derivatives are divided fairly evenly between offensive odors and pleasant or neutral ones. If one then turns to the *Spenser Concordance,* similar proportions are to be found. The honest word "stink," with its derivatives, is used by Shakespeare nineteen times (six of these cases have to do with the populace); by Spenser it is used twelve times. The proportion is thus higher in Spenser. From these rapid, but highly representative comparisons and from simple observation of one's own verbal usage, it would appear that Miss Spurgeon's case for Shakespeare's high sensitivity to offensive smell is exaggerated: that he has no more of a tendency to dwell upon the odoriferous, except in describing the populace, than has Spenser or any other normal person who divides his remarks about equally between good and evil.

As for the belief that Shakespeare's theme of the "rank-scented many" amounted to nothing more than a literary or dramatic convention, there is at least this to be said: it is not discoverable as a theme in Shakespeare's sources or in the manifold contemporary assaults upon the populace which will be discussed in Chapter IV. Nor do contemporary plays having mob scenes or dealing with mob action exhibit the device: *Jack Straw, Sir Thomas More, Edward IV, Sejanus, Appius and Virginia,* and *Philaster* are examples.[21] While the idea may occasionally be expressed in literary or dramatic form, there is no reiteration of it; it does not stand out as a refrain. It must be recognized that wherever there is popular political assemblage in Shakespeare this derisive theme occurs. It is scarcely a dramatic convention, except in Shake-

21 See Chapter V for further discussion of these plays.

speare, and it is not easily explainable as a dramatic expedient.

When Brandes' data are thus amplified and then checked by comparison with the plays of other dramatists and with other Shakespearean material, we are at least able to say that the personal feelings of Shakespeare for which he argues are as well demonstrated as any personal trait of an author can be in the absence of autobiographical statement or testimony of reliable observers. Repetitive use of the stench motif and the fact that it is not derived from dramatic convention and necessity, or from sources, or from the requirement of characterization are matters hard to ignore. Moreover, when it is found that in two prominent episodes Shakespeare proceeds from this theme into satire upon audiences and actors, there is at least a suggestion of Brandes' conclusion that his revulsion arose from an artist's reaction to the public. We may be certain, however, that Brandes was wrong if he meant to ascribe the phenomenon to one cause; if we can be sure of anything in the devious practice of inferential biography it is that causes of personal antagonism lie hidden in complex amalgam with other motives and that the explanation of these traits is suspect if it is monistic. We are driven to speculate upon the line in Sonnet 111 on "public means which public manners breeds," upon Shakespeare's association with Southampton, upon his status as a propertied man and his urge to be one of the gentry, and upon his response to official publicity adverse to the populace, which will be discussed later. These are but a few of the issues which must be met should one choose to bring Shakespeare's personal traits into the picture. For such reasons, while it has been necessary to examine this question, it will be much more rewarding to treat the problem henceforth as an impersonal one, to be concerned, not with Shakespeare's private antagonisms, but with public receptivity to the theme of *demos* in his plays and with some of the social causes which underlay that receptivity.

This, however, is not to dismiss Brandes, as modern interpretation has been so prone to do. Some misgivings have
been noted concerning the school of criticism which looks
upon Shakespeare behavioristically, as though the only biographical facts to be derived from his art were conditioned
patterns of behavior in a framework of convention and
tradition. Undeniably, this way of thinking was a reaction
away from excesses common to romantic interpreters, of
whom Brandes is one, but the reaction itself has moved
steadily toward another variety of romanticism: a view of
the Elizabethan period as a kind of golden age in which the
motives of playwrights, at least insofar as we may discuss
them, were objectively simple, standardized, and uncluttered
with idiosyncracy. Stereotyping and a passion for the pal-
pable datum can in the end be equivalent to romantic nostal-
gia for simplicity; realism calls for more than this, for a
willingness to handle imaginative hypotheses together with
method and discipline in doing it.

THE ATTACK UPON SHAKESPEARE

Brandes' analysis of Shakespeare and the populace, however realistic and unpleasant, was not intended as a critical
attack, but as a critical description; there is in it, moreover,
a suggestion that Brandes himself found the antidemocratic
themes of Shakespeare natural enough for an artist and
scarcely uncongenial to a sensitive person. The views which
follow are of a different order; they are those of noteworthy
people who have condemned Shakespeare's social bias with
little reservation. One of the first of these was Hazlitt, who
declared that the "whole dramatic moral of *Coriolanus* is
that those who have little shall have less. . . . The people
are poor, therefore they ought to be starved. They are slaves,
therefore they ought to be beaten. They work hard, therefore they ought to be treated like beasts of burden." [22] To
Walt Whitman, Shakespeare's plays were "poisonous to the

[22] *Characters in Shakespeare's Plays* (Everyman edition), p. 57.

idea of the pride and dignity of the common people, the life-blood of democracy." [23] Professor Thaler, however, has shown that Whitman's ideas on this subject underwent modification more favorable to Shakespeare,[24] and Professor Falk has called attention to Whitman's interesting notion of a Shakespeare who satirized feudalism so subtly that even the Cade and Joan of Arc episodes might have been written to deflect courtly suspicion of subversive ideas! [25] Whitman was apparently both uneasy and ingenious in attempting to meet the problem, and it will appear that in this he hardly stood alone.

Ernest Crosby regretted that he could find in Shakespeare no instances of "serious and estimable behaviour on the part of the individuals representing the lower classes, or of considerate treatment of them on the part of their betters." Crosby complained further of the ignominious roles assigned to plebeians in Shakespeare, as well as of the humiliating names given to them, and concluded that "having a poor opinion of the lower classes taken man by man, Shakespeare thinks . . . still worse of them taken *en masse,* and at his hands a crowd of plain workingmen fares worst of all." [26] Tolstoy seconded this position,[27] and George Bernard Shaw denounced "Shakespeare's snobbery," "his vulgar prejudice," "his ignorance," and "his weakness and incoherence as a thinker." [28] Nor has this point of view been unexpressed in

[23] "Democratic Vistas," in *Complete Prose Works* (New York, G. P. Putnam's Sons, 1902), V, 90.
[24] *Shakespeare and Democracy* (Knoxville, University of Tennessee Press, 1941), pp. 45–61.
[25] Robert P. Falk, "Shakespeare's Place in Walt Whitman's America," *Shakespeare Association Bulletin,* XXVII (April, 1942), 86–96.
[26] "Shakespeare's Working Classes," *The Craftsman* (April, 1903), pp. 35, 37, 43. *Shakespeare's Attitude toward the Working Classes* (1907), p. 140. Cited by Tupper, below.
[27] *Shakespeare* (1906), with an introduction by G. B. Shaw. Contains Crosby's essay in an appendix.
[28] In a letter to Tchertkoff on Tolstoy's opinions of Shakespeare. Quoted in Joseph McCabe, *George Bernard Shaw, a Critical Study* (London, 1914), p. 148.

times closer to our own, for Professor Thaler has reported that Carl Sandburg, in a public lecture in 1938, deemed the work of Shakespeare to be of negligible importance for a democratic people.[29]

There is no real need for extended comment upon these opinions; they have been of value in forcing the issue against orthodox criticism, but with no intention of considering them lightly, they may be dismissed as anachronistic. That Shakespeare was not a prototype of William Morris or of Norman Thomas can readily be demonstrated, and it is sometimes a fact worth demonstration to those who celebrate Shakespeare's timeless love of all humanity. Beyond being a corrective irritant, however, the argument is a little fatuous; as well might one criticize Queen Elizabeth for not having been a social worker. In any event, those of us who are liberals and democrats would do well to confine our spleen to modern totalitarians.

MARXIST INTERPRETATION

There may be some surprise that Marxist critics of Shakespeare have failed to join in the condemnation made by Tolstoy, Crosby, Shaw, and others. Of the four who will be considered, none criticizes Shakespeare for representing the populace unfavorably; in fact the three who deal specifically with Shakespeare are fulsome in their approval of his position.

The first of these characteristic interpreters is A. A. Smirnov, who wishes especially to avoid anachronism in judging Shakespeare by standards of modern democracy. Smirnov's reasoning is that Shakespeare's contempt for the populace was intelligent, because reactionary or what may be called neo-feudal factions of the sixteenth and seventeenth centuries made effective use of a willing rabble against the rising middle

---

[29] *Shakespeare and Democracy*, p. 9. Professor Thaler also cites E. A. Robinson in this vein.

class; aversion to the populace under these conditions, he declares, was progressive. In brief, revolution, not of the mass, but of the middle class against aristocratic privilege (the rise of bourgeois capitalism) was in motion, and, according to Smirnov, it is with reference to this historical change and to no other that Shakespeare's progressivism should be estimated.[30]

In agreement with Smirnov, Donald Morrow, an American interpreter, believes that Shakespeare gave expression to the nationalistic and middle-class spirit opposed to Catholic and feudal elements. His affirmation of the new bourgeois social class logically included contempt for the democratic idea which Morrow, like Smirnov, explains or excuses on the ground that "the lower classes then were historically not so important as they were later to become." [31]

George Thomson accentuates this position so far as to write that "Shakespeare in his time was a revolutionary force," today ironically stripped of revolutionary fervor by the very middle class whose original militancy he expressed. Mr. Thomson, however, introduces complexity into the question when he notes that with the accession of James I, the monarchy ceased to be a focus of revolutionary middle-class culture. "The change had a profound effect upon Shakespeare. All his great tragedies were written under the new regime," and in most of them "he is subconsciously, but plainly, preoccupied with the issue [of divine right] raised by James I in his struggle against the bourgeoisie," even to the extent in *Coriolanus* of voicing "his fear of the forces which, if it is to overthrow the monarchy, the bourgeoisie will have to call into action." [32] Here it will be noted that Thomson runs contrary to his co-Marxist Smirnov, who as-

[30] *Shakespeare; a Marxist Interpretation* (New York, The Liberal Press, 1936), pp. 59–60.

[31] *Where Shakespeare Stood* (Milwaukee, The Casanova Press, 1935). See especially pp. 70, 77, and 81.

[32] *Marxism and Poetry* (New York, International Publishers, 1946), pp. 55 ff., 64.

sumes that the populace typified in *Coriolanus* was called
into action, not by the bourgeoisie; but by the reactionary
monarchy.

The disagreement here over the role of the populace is
complicated by another Marxist interpretation of the 1640
revolution, an outgrowth of social conflicts present in Shakespeare's day. Opposed to Smirnov, it is stated in one place [33]
that the common people were not allied with royalists against
the new middle class; "on the contrary, the popular parties
proved to be the King's most militant opponents, far more
vigorous and ruthless and thorough-going than the bourgeoisie itself." Emphasized also is fear felt by the gentry of
"threats of a peasant revolt such as had shaken the midlands
in 1607." [34] Supporting Smirnov's theory, however, is the
included quotation from Baxter, a contemporary: "most of
the poorest of the people, whom the others call the rabble,
did follow the gentry and were for the king." [35] Also in par-
tial agreement with Smirnov's interpretation is a diagnosis
of the Leveler faction: because the Levelers looked back to
precapitalist peasant stability, they were "bound to be de-
feated." Indeed, in the Leveler program there was "a trend
that is 'medieval' and even reactionary." [36]

In these variant Marxist estimates of the populace as both
progressive and reactionary, and in the divergent reasons
Marxists give for placing Shakespeare on the progressive
side, there is some pointed contradiction. This, however, is
not so fundamental as it seems; either Marxist attitude
toward the populace could be partly right, for both factions
in sixteenth- and seventeenth-century struggles depended
upon popular support, as any faction must. The problem to
Marxists is which faction, if either, the enigmatic Shakespeare thought stigmatized by support from the populace.

In attempting to resolve this complication, some help may

[33] *The English Revolution 1640*, ed. by Christopher Hill (London, Lawrence
and Wishart, Ltd., 1940), p. 13. The Marxist Text Book Series.
[34] *Ibid.*, p. 55.   [35] *Ibid.*, p. 18.   [36] *Ibid.*, p. 30.

be derived from Marxist interpreters themselves. Christopher Hill points out that until about 1590 the interests of the Tudor monarchy in the struggle against Spain, the Catholics, and remnants of feudalism, coincided with interests of the rising middle class. As feudalism declined, however, its representatives became more and more parasitical upon the monarchy; the middle classes, on the other hand, found the monarchy progressively more antagonistic.[37] If this is true, condemnation of baronial instability in Shakespeare's history plays of the early 1590's could be described as progressive doctrine from the standpoint of the rising middle class, whereas by the time of *Troilus and Cressida,* Ulysses' speech condemning the same kind of instability could have been reactionary from such a standpoint because of antimiddle-class connotations which by that time had become attached to sentiments expressed in it. Were Mr. Hill's formula applied to the present issue, it might be inferred that Shakespeare's similar attack on the populace in the early Cade scenes was progressive from the middle-class point of view, *circa* 1590, and his later attack on the populace in *Coriolanus* reactionary from the middle-class point of view, *circa* 1607. This is complicated, but conceivable if the earlier "progressives" favored social stability, while the later ones had come to view it as reactionary.

Such a balanced disposition of the issue would imply some paradox, complexity, and dynamism in its social-historical outlook, and the Marxist critics are at least to be congratulated for standing almost alone on that score among interpreters of the Shakespearean social theme. It is with no impulse to dismiss their case that the writer disagrees with them.

Evidence for this disagreement is found in Chapter IV, in which it will appear that thoughout the 1590's and later, social leveling, democratic factionalism, and mob disorder

[37] *Ibid.,* pp. 39–40.

were insisted upon by conservative spokesmen as necessary consequences of the nonconformist movement, whether moderate or extremist. If Shakespeare's projection of mob rule fits into this picture, it must follow that it was anti-Puritan or "unprogressive," and that Marxist claims for Shakespeare's pre-eminence as a spokesman of middle-class ideals must be challenged. The Marxist view of Shakespeare as "a healthy, well poised, sceptical, melioristic humanist, somewhat to the left of the centre of advanced bourgeois opinion," [38] will be found less convincing than an alternative Marxist view: "Shakespeare's tragic outlook on the world was consequential upon his being the dramatic expression of the feudal aristocracy which in Elizabeth's day had lost [its] former dominating position." [39] The latter view, however, is distinctly a minority one among Marxist interpreters.

Of Marxist critics in general it may be said that, while their inferences are based upon vivid conception of the social conflict of Shakespeare's own day, they are nevertheless too pat and ingenious, either in placing Shakespeare in the forefront of progressivism or in offering reasons at once materialistic and monistic to explain whatever position they assign to him. That individual Marxist interpreters contradict one another, however, is not too important; so do non-Marxist interpreters.

TRADITIONAL INTERPRETATION

Since the time of Coleridge there has grown a critical literature rich in apology for Shakespearean scenes in which the populace is satirized. Except for a few, who will be described later, most interpreters have not been concerned with dramatists other than Shakespeare, with nondramatic writers, or with social conditions of the Tudor and Stuart periods;

[38] T. A. Jackson, *International Literature*, No. 2 (1936). Quoted in L. C. Knight, *Drama and Society in the Age of Jonson* (London, Chatto and Windus, 1937), p. 9.
[39] "Shakespeare through Russian Eyes," a condensation and free translation of two articles by Lunacharsky and Kogan, *The Listener*, Dec. 27, 1934. This quotation is also from Knight, *op. cit.*

they have largely considered Shakespeare in isolation, and have emphasized qualities of mellowness and reconciliation. Characteristic writers of this school have celebrated his good humor and tolerance in depiction of humble individuals and his unwillingness to suffer gladly the scoundrels and fools of high station. Standard exemplars of the orthodox view are Coleridge, Dowden, Bradley, Tannenbaum, Tolman, R. W. Chambers, Wood, Thaler, and Palmer. Were this a bibliographical survey, a dozen more names would be necessary to complete the list of those who have written specifically to the issue; if parenthetical asides by writers upon other subjects were to be enumerated, an exhaustive search through Shakespeare annals would be necessary, for the problem seems to arise in the most unexpected places. The uniformity of traditional criticism will be apparent, however, to anyone who reads several of the commentators just named, and for this purpose references appear in the notes to this chapter.[40]

The orthodox brief for humanity and sympathy bestowed by Shakespeare upon individuals of low caste appears in a short quotation from Bradley:

[Shakespeare's] poor and humble are, almost without exception, sound and sweet at heart, faithful and pitiful. . . . He has no respect for the plainer and simpler kind of people as politicians, but a great respect and regard for their hearts.[41]

[40] Coleridge, *Lectures and Notes on Shakespeare* (London, 1900), pp. 281–282, 309–310. Dowden, *Shakespeare; A Critical Study of His Mind and Art* (New York, Harper and Bros., no date), pp. 286–289. Bradley, *Coriolanus*. Second Annual British Academy Shakespeare Lecture, 1912. Tannenbaum, "Shakespeare's Caste Prejudices," in *Shakespearean Scraps and Other Fragments* (New York, Columbia University Press, 1933), pp. 153–176. Tolman, "Is Shakespeare Aristocratic?" *PMLA*, XXIX (1914), 277–298, especially 289 ff. R. W. Chambers, "The Expression of Ideas—Particularly Political Ideas," in *Shakespeare's Hand in the Play of Sir Thomas More* (Cambridge, Cambridge University Press, 1923), pp. 142–187, particularly 165 ff. Wood, "Shakespeare and the Plebs," in *Essays and Studies by Members of the English Association*, XVIII (1933), 53–73. Thaler, *Shakespeare and Democracy*. Palmer, *Political Characters of Shakespeare* (London, The Macmillan Company, 1945), pp. 250–310.

[41] *Shakespearean Tragedy* (London, The Macmillan Company, 1929), p. 326 and note.

No exception can be taken to this statement as it stands, for it is not only perfectly true but also humane, and any appraisal of Shakespeare which lacked it would be a narrow one. The trouble arises from the use to which the truism is put, for the traditional critics are not content to let it stand, but employ it either to allay democratic misgivings of their own concerning Shakespeare's satire upon the multitude or to refute the attackers of Shakespeare already reviewed. Reduced to brevity, their reasoning is that because Shakespeare shows high regard for certain lowly individuals he is essentially democratic, and because he is essentially democratic in that respect his treatment of man in the mass apparent in the Cade scenes, *Julius Caesar,* and *Coriolanus* is explained away, compensated for, or irrelevant.

This by no means follows. The observation exemplified by Bradley, when used to deny somehow the charge that Shakespeare's plays are sternly aristocratic, is as puzzling as it is winsome. Engaging plebeians like Adam and the various fools are complimented within severely aristocratic limits; Adam is esteemed in *As You Like It* largely because he recognizes and accepts his place in the social scale. But let such a character cross the line, as do Oswald the steward in *Lear* and Malvolio in *Twelfth Night,* or let him be Jack Cade threatening traditional rule. There benevolence and sentiment cease; spleen and satire begin—all of it very aristocratic and very Elizabethan.

It could be added that even benevolent Shakespearean portraits of the lowly are hardly democratic in their conception, for when judged by Elizabethan standards or by any others they exhibit one of the most aristocratic traditions, that of *noblesse oblige.* Surely there is nothing alarmingly republican at any time in a sympathy for gnomic bumpkins, dutiful soldiers, or faithful servants. This, however, need not be insisted upon, for there is another issue which is more central. What we really need is a definition of democracy applicable both to Shakespeare's world and to our own. Tentatively, it could be said that democracy implies respect for the ordinary man and faith in his political judgment. It must be added, however, that a democratic outlook requires more than this, that it is essentially an attitude held with reference, not to individuals, but to aggregations or masses of people. The definition might thus be enlarged: democracy is based upon respect for the common man and faith in his political judgment, a respect and faith which are not diminished when common men join together for purposes of social reform. This does not mean that one of democratic faith rejoices in every popular program which may materialize, that he believes popular sovereignty can never be tyrannous, or that he uncritically approves of pressure groups merely because they have the sanction of large numbers. But it does imply several attitudes which are affirmative enough and clear-cut enough to separate believers in democracy from verbal sympathizers. It implies, for one thing, that a believer in democracy, although privately irked at some pressure groups, will prefer a group of that kind with large mass following to one which seeks privilege for the few; it implies also that he will not be frightened or uneasy over mass political pressure simply because it comes from the mass; it implies finally that although a democrat may recognize excess and error as occasional results of popular rule, he will nevertheless believe that popular sovereignty in the long run yields greater general benefit than any alternative system.

Now comes the difficulty. A good enough test of democratic principle when applied to the twentieth century, one might say, but what right have we to apply it to the work of Shakespeare or other Elizabethans? What busy nonsense is this which would ask how Tudor Englishmen felt about majority rule; is it not like asking what they thought of the direct primary or the C.I.O.?

The answer is that no one asks what Tudor Englishmen

thought of modern applications of this definition of democracy. One asks, instead, how some of them measure up to it against a background of their own political issues. But were there political issues facing Elizabethans to which the definition could apply? It is sometimes forgotten that the movement toward the Commonwealth was political as well as religious; this information is offered with no air of discovery, but as a reminder that regardless of what moderns may think of sixteenth- and seventeenth-century nonconformity, it was attacked in Shakespeare's day as a dangerous child of "Popularity," which threatened both social stability and privilege. No matter how aloof we may be from this state of affairs, people of Shakespeare's time were told that religious dissent, if it took root with the populace, would level gradation, destroy private property, and culminate in anarchy. This estimate may appear extreme in the absence of evidence which cannot be offered until the next chapter, but if accepted tentatively it will make possible an Elizabethan application of the definition of democracy previously offered. Elizabethans who made or were led to believe accusations of leveling against nonconformists and therefore opposed moderate reform were undemocratically inclined according to standards of their time. And contemporaries of Shakespeare who either did not fear or did not believe the leveling charges and tolerated or favored nonconformity were democratically inclined according to sixteenth-century standards.

But even if the truth of this is granted, what has it all to do with the plays of Shakespeare? The Cade scenes, *Julius Caesar,* and *Coriolanus* are not plays about religious nonconformists or even about peaceful citizens banded together in a cause; they are plays about mobs. "If Shakespeare is severe on mobs we Americans must be the last ones to find fault with him for that; his mobs are never so ferocious, unreasonable, or debased as those that darken the pages of our annals." [42] This observation of Professor Tannenbaum would seem to dispose of the question. What bearing upon democracy has an Elizabethan play about a mob, or a modern play about a mob, when we all know that mob action has been employed to repress democratic decency the world over?

This challenge is a genuine one. Before it leads, however, into classification of *Julius Caesar* as a democratic play because of implied contempt for lynchers of Cinna the poet, another point of view might be entertained. We can certify the democracy of those who detest lynch mobs or bands of brown-shirted bravoes, but what shall we say of those in our midst who likewise hate mobs and sense a kind of mob-threat in every assemblage from a popular political party to a picket line? There may be some doubt about their essential democracy. Similarly, if it is found that many Elizabethans, including some dramatists, looked upon popular movements or popular assemblages as mob rule *per se*, while others, also including dramatists, took a different view,[43] the issue may then assume another nature. It may be that the problem is not whether Shakespeare had contempt for mobs (there can be little doubt of that), but whether there were reasons for public interest in theatrical mob scenes, and whether there were causes for dramatic portrayal of popular movements in the guise of mob anarchy, mob stupidity, or mob terror. This, perhaps, is the issue, and effort will shortly be made to meet it. For the present, however, there must be further scrutiny of traditional interpretation.

Except for questioning its relation to mob scenes, the traditional claim for Shakespeare's generosity to lowly individuals has been admitted. It has raised squarely the problem of defining democracy in Elizabethan terms and in such a way that masses rather than individuals are included. The ortho-

---

[42] Tannenbaum, *op. cit.*, p. 172.   [43] See the discussion in Chapter V.

dox view, however, does not stop with this issue of humble individuals; there are further questions raised by almost all traditional apologists.

One of these issues rests upon a fact hardly requiring demonstration: that pretentiousness, stupidity, corruption, and rebellion are exhibited in Shakespeare's plays quite as often by aristocrats as by commoners, and that the dramatist's implied disapproval is bestowed equally among both factions for the same sins and shortcomings. The plays thus are said to present a neutral balance favoring neither aristocracy nor commonalty. A number of interesting objections to this appraisal could be made; chief among them would be to recognize that in Shakespeare it is righteous aristocracy which is always placed in ethical opposition both to unworthy aristocracy and to the assembled commons. Complication can be avoided, however, if it is admitted readily that the orthodox claim is true, that Shakespeare's humanity was great enough for him to have seen folly distributed among all classes and virtue residing in no one caste. Had it not been for this, had Shakespeare been a narrow propagandist or a persistent grinder of axes, the question would now have little flavor and interest. We ought to agree once and for all that in Shakespeare there is fusion of right and wrong which is humanity —not at its best or worst, but at its average. But this almost patronizing concession of greatness will hardly lead to solution of the problem; that Shakespeare is realistic about fools or knaves in high place is hardly a fact which explains the Cade scenes. If, for example, a modern novelist damns capital and labor equally, his contempt for one is not a very good explanation of his contempt for the other; it is just another fact to be explained. Nor does such catholicity show him necessarily to have breadth of view and rich understanding, an attribute some assign to Shakespeare because of the "plague on both your houses" theme and little else.

Another, and a much more cogent point of standard criticism is that the fumbling of the plebs in *Julius Caesar* and *Coriolanus* is no real reflection upon their intelligence, especially since they are misled by politicians like Antony and the tribunes. R. W. Chambers observes that the world has never been able to make up its mind upon the course of action taken by Brutus, "yet we blame the handicraft men of Rome because they cannot decide directly; ay, and briefly; ay and wisely." [44] Likewise, who can pass judgment upon the citizenry in *Coriolanus* for failing to be Lycurguses when the best brains of history have not met successfully the problem of economic scarcity and class conflict. Chambers shows that in *Coriolanus* the citizens, although not bright, are clearly charitable; they want to understand, they want to make allowances, but the arrogance of Coriolanus and the duplicity of the tribunes combine to deprive them of all opportunity to act sensibly.[45] The dramatist, moreover, sympathizes with the citizens and reserves his scorn for the tribunes; in fact it may be admitted with Chambers that Shakespeare "hated and despised the tribunes in *Coriolanus* with a bitterness which he rarely felt towards any of his creatures." [46]

There is an interpretation of these facts, however, which runs contrary to Chambers' provocative analysis: it begins with ready admission that Shakespeare's citizenry cannot be blamed for failure to be statesmen, that they are duped by demagogues, and that they are not cold in their class antagonisms, but warmly impulsive. Yet if attention is paid to the tone and the dramatic emphasis (see Chapter II) with which Shakespeare implements his presentation of the multitude— in short, if we try to imagine the plays as they must have been staged—we derive a conception of the common people as not whimsically perplexed, but in the main ridiculous, as not simply duped, but perversely prone to be so, and as not merely impulsive, but essentially violent. And significantly,

[44] *Shakespeare's Hand in the Play of Sir Thomas More*, pp. 173–174.
[45] *Ibid.*, pp. 168–172.   [46] *Ibid.*, p. 168.

they are doomed to show these traits without cessation or variation. When Chambers writes of Shakespearean mobs as perplexed by enigmas neither they nor we will ever penetrate, he writes of them as one might write of Hamlet. But if a truism may be pardoned, from Hamlet's efforts to resolve perplexity comes an awareness that human dignity is being served; from the perplexity of Shakespeare's mobs comes an impression that massed humanity is simian. More than this, if the misleading of Shakespeare's populace is charged to popular leaders, we are still left with a populace which will be misled again and again. We may agree that the mob scenes are robust, comic, at times complicated, and not ill-naturedly written. But we can assent to this without entering an ethical haze in which satirical emphasis means nothing more than gusto and warm understanding. Above all else, we could try to stop blaming anyone for the defection of Shakespeare's commoners, whether it be the tribunes, Antony, Cade alias Mortimer, or Shakespeare himself. We could then attempt to understand why mob scenes were so consistently staged, but before any interpretation is possible, the scenes must be accepted at their dramatic face value.

The next issue is one which is raised by nearly unanimous agreement of traditional interpreters. It is that Shakespeare's plays, because they are plays, present political ideas only through characters, and that the political ideas are thus largely confined in function to character portrayal. This is taken to mean that Shakespeare does not editorialize upon political subjects or other subjects, but enigmatically allows Coriolanus, the tribunes, Jack Cade, or others to voice and to act out points of view characteristic of their limited and frankly biased personalities. Any student of Shakespeare is aware of the fallacy which traps those who seek a "message" from dramatic writing as though it were a special form of lyric utterance, but avoidance of this fallacy can be extended to unreasonable lengths. One questionable overuse of the precaution was suggested in an earlier discussion of the traditional attitude opposed to Brandes. There is no need here, however, to complicate the question by introducing Shakespeare's private political feelings, for although it may be agreed that his characters do not speak his mind, the traditional inference from this need not be conceded. The traditional critic does more than to warn against attributing sentiments of Shakespeare's characters to the dramatist himself; he habitually minimizes the function of a play in carrying political meaning or doctrine to an audience, and this he likewise justifies by the premise that ideas in a play are expressed by characters and have little significance beyond that of character drawing. The most recent commentator upon the meaning of *Coriolanus* considers very realistically the grasp of politics implicit in the play; he defends, for example, the tribunes' lack of disinterest, a target of pious attack since the time of Johnson, by reminding us that leaders of a political cause cannot afford to be disinterested. And yet, after this and further extensive discussion of political tensions dramatized by Shakespeare, Mr. Palmer concludes upon this note:

We are here confronted with the paradox which lies in wait for all who study with attention the political plays of Shakespeare. "Coriolanus," as we have seen, is more exclusively concerned with politics than any other play he ever wrote. The politics are nevertheless in the last analysis incidental. Shakespeare is intent on persons, not on public affairs. His interest, when he writes of Coriolanus, as when he writes of Brutus or Henry or Richard, is in a human character who happens also to be a politician. There are more politics to be found in his plays than in those of any other dramatic writer. We invariably find, however, that his theme, as it takes shape and moves to a climax, is not essentially a political problem but the adventure of a human spirit. We discover, in fact, that Shakespeare, who wrote more genuinely political plays than any other dramatist before or since, is only indirectly concerned with the political principles and ideas in which they abound. Hazlitt refers to the arguments in "Coriolanus" for and against aristocracy and democracy. There are no such arguments. There are only aristocrats and democrats.[47]

[47] *Political Characters of Shakespeare*, pp. 250–310. The quotation is from pp. 308–309. Reprinted by permission of The Macmillan Company.

To this the great majority of Shakespeare's interpreters cry assent. It is very difficult, in fact, to do otherwise, provided the literal meaning of the peroration alone is considered; how could one construe even *Coriolanus* to be a voter's manual presenting arguments "for and against" a political idea or course of action? It is true that there are those who view politics in Shakespeare's plays as something much more than incidental, just as there are those who discern little in a well-contrived novel but juxtaposition, *a la* morality play, of good and evil. Orthodox criticism, however, scores a lonely and platitudinous triumph when it seeks out such opposition, and no one who responds to Shakespeare's extraordinary presentation of the human equation need linger to witness the encounter; we do not have to be reminded that Shakespeare is first of all a dramatist.

The most direct way of heeding Mr. Palmer's warning would be to agree that politics is but incidental in *Coriolanus* and proceed to comment upon the incidental. By this course of action, however, one would not join issue with the real meaning of such interpretation and would therefore ignore an interesting tendency of literary criticism. For the importance of the orthodox view here lies in its implication that politics in literature is something slightly off-color or unworthy at best of a first-class craftsman. One wonders what the dramatist who conceived a great cycle of historical plays based upon the consequences of Richard II's dethronement would have thought of this. Fundamentally it represents a kind of prudishness; the traditional attitude toward politics in Shakespeare resembles the excuses made for sex in literature by those to whom it is offensive but who do not wish to be thought puritanical in the invidious sense. Interpreting the novels of D. H. Lawrence, for example, such critics are quick to declare that while sex is a dominant theme, it is, nevertheless, allowed to flourish mainly as a powerful and legitimate motivation of the characters. And these critics are right, of course, in everything but the inevitable implication that Lawrence was less interested in sex than in characterization. Mr. Palmer's statement may be tested by changing it so that *Measure for Measure* is substituted for *Coriolanus* and "sex" for "politics." We should then have a declaration that while *Measure for Measure* is perhaps more exclusively concerned with sex than any other play of Shakespeare, sex nevertheless, "in the last analysis," is but incidental. Shakespeare is intent on persons, not sex, and while the latter is posed as a problem, the play is still not a problem play, but an "adventure in the human spirit." Instead of arguments for and against chastity and profligacy, there are only characters who are chaste and those who are profligate. To which, it would seem, the only observation possible is that it would be difficult to write a play about sex without having people in it or to write a play about people without having some sex in it.

To return hastily to politics, the majority of critics may legitimately be asked to clarify the standard apology. Apparently we are to gather from it that politics, instead of being the inevitable concern of civilized men who wish to live together in communities, is a somewhat intrusive pursuit and that a dramatist of stature will subordinate it to a higher aim, the exploration of human individuality. But what does "subordinate" mean? Does it mean the presentation of politics in such a manner that audiences will ignore political problems in favor of character motivation? If so, one expects audiences to do something unusual. Or does subordination of politics mean that the dramatist merely refrains from preaching or from "sociological" analysis. If so, something has been prescribed which any good dramatist intuitively prescribes for himself. Finally, are we to understand from orthodox critics that Shakespeare believed monistically that the content of literary art should be subsumed under characterization? If so, they have come out roundly for intuition concerning

Shakespeare's private convictions and have closed their eyes to one of the sternest warnings of orthodox criticism itself.

There is, perhaps, a more objective way of considering the matter by assuming that dramatists are pluralists who do not consistently classify their techniques under a main heading, that they are well aware of the tendency of audiences to be just as responsive to ethical issues—politics is a part of ethics—as to characterization. And dramatists know, moreover, that audiences do not require for ethical interpretation the kind of summation scene which Mr. Palmer implies that Shakespeare would have inserted had his intentions been heavily moralistic.[48] In the absence of other evidence, the test of a dramatist's intentions could be the same as the test of intention applied by the courts. In law a man is presumed to intend "the natural and probable consequences" of his acts. So if a practiced dramatist writes a play such as *Coriolanus*, he should be presumed to know that popular audiences are prone to see "issues" in it and that whether they find profound characterization or not, they rarely consider the latter to be more significant than the problem. One might go further: when a practiced dramatist writes such a play, he may be presumed to know that those in the audience who do not love the populace are going to rejoice in doctrinaire fashion over verbal assaults on the multitude from the protagonist and from Menenius, and that one of the last things these prejudiced spectators will consider is the possibility that the diatribes may be largely for purposes of character drawing. Finally, if a dramatist accompanies such material with the techniques of emphasis discussed in Chapter II, he may be presumed to intend the natural and probable audience responses which these techniques have customarily induced. What were Shakespeare's private feelings or reservations as he did these things? We do not know, any more than a judge knows what were the private hesitations of A when

[48] *Political Characters of Shakespeare,* p. 309.

he wrote a letter to B, and instructs the jury that it is to construe A's intent from the natural interpretation of the letter
by B. If we did know Shakespeare's private designs, qualms,
or enthusiasms as he wrote these plays, we should have a
very interesting story. But even if we had the story, we should
still be confronted with a problem of audience response to
the plays and of the social tensions which elicited that response.

Two more currents of standard interpretation remain,
both of them characterized, not by apology for Shakespeare's
political plays, but rather by commendable attempts to relate them to contemporary background. The first of these
would relate Shakespeare's social themes to standard Elizabethan political theory, and we need consider but one of the
more recent investigators in this field. Professor Draper proposes "to investigate the plays for reflections not of current
political event, but of current political theory." [49] Briefly,
such interpretations are concerned with various theories of
monarchy and the state current in a century notable for its
output in a field we now call political science. Among other
treatises, Professor Draper is concerned with Smith, *De
republica Anglorum* (1583); Floyd, *The Picture of a Perfit
Commonwealth* (1600); the political writings of James I;
and G. More, *Principles for Yong Princes*. A basic discussion
of political theory during this period is to be found in J. W.
Allen's *Political Thought in the Sixteenth Century,* and a
great deal of this material supplements and complements
Shakespeare's theme of social gradation. A knowledge of it,
moreover, is indispensable, but the explanation it furnishes
of Elizabethan political plays may be insufficient. Political
treatises, even in popularized form, are hardly primary background materials, for they are in need of the same explanation required by political plays themselves. Out of what

49 "Political Themes of Shakespeare's Later Plays," *JEGP*, XXXV (1936),
61-93.

social ferment did they grow? One does not adequately explain a conservative modern novel such as *Prodigal Parents* or a left-wing play such as *Awake and Sing* by citations from a book on political theory; instead, one needs to consider all three—novel, play, and book—in the light of social dislocation during recent years which has made them timely to contemporary readers.

In no sense, however, is investigation of sixteenth-century political theory to be underrated; contributions such as those of Professor Draper in periodical form and of Professors Campbell, Phillips, and Tillyard in book form [50] are invaluable. The present investigation is but an attempt to continue from the point at which historical political theory may cease to explain.

Last to be considered among traditional schools of criticism is one which places Shakespeare effectively within a literary and dramatic tradition. Disturbed as early as 1912 by complex and varied interpretations, Professor Tupper demonstrated that "the Shakespearean mob has its genesis and justification not in any individual aloofness or in personal hostility, but in contemporary history and sentiment, in literary tradition, in the Elizabethan dramatic convention, and in the poet's sources, both English and classical." [51] Mr. Tupper has called attention to a body of Elizabethan plays which eliminates any notion that Shakespeare's personal attitudes are very important in the problem, for such plays clearly suggest that Elizabethan plebeians were fair game for many a dramatist of the time. Historical scholarship in literature, however, is often to be questioned when it assumes that a showing of literary or dramatic convention explains adequately what we wish to know. The tone of Hamlet's

[50] Lily B. Campbell, *Shakespeare's "Histories," Mirrors of Elizabethan Policy* (San Marino, Calif., The Huntington Library, 1947). J. E. Phillips, Jr., *The State in Shakespeare's Greek and Roman Plays* (New York, Columbia University Press, 1940). E. M. W. Tillyard, *Shakespeare's History Plays* (New York, The Macmillan Company, 1946).

[51] "The Shakespearean Mob," *PMLA*, XXVII (1912), 486–523. The quotation is on p. 490.

soliloquies, for example, cannot be satisfactorily explained by Elizabethan conventions of pessimism, melancholy, and malcontentism. As well might we try to account for Dreiser's pessimism and determinism by pointing to the same qualities in Hardy and others, and while it is true that traditional themes often flourish by imitation, even hackneyed literary motifs will have other immediate causes. When an Elizabethan dramatist assaults the mob with a formula of two parts horse-play and one of magisterial calm, when he calls upon heaven to certify hierarchy in all things from earth, air, fire, and water to peers of the realm, it is likely that he is activated not only by other writers but also by the state of England. In short, the relationship of literary themes to actual social disturbance is hardly lessened by showing that the literary themes were conventional ones; it may be said, in fact, that attitudes which have become conventional are especially related to social issues for the obvious reason that social undercurrents most commonly appear in conventions of belief and behavior. The dramatic tradition of which Shakespeare's mob scenes are a part will continue, however, to be a rewarding field of research. That the present study depends heavily upon it will be made apparent in later discussion, for although one may be occupied principally with social backgrounds, they cannot be separated from dramatic tradition, especially if there are variations within the tradition.

In this chapter it has been suggested that Shakespeare's theme of the populace cannot be explained by ascribing it to his private social views; that attacks upon Shakespeare the reactionary are as profitless as praise for Shakespeare the progressive; and that the various forms of apology for anti-democratic satire in Shakespeare are unrewarding. It has also been pointed out that the denial of doctrinaire elements in Shakespeare amounts to a truism which contributes little to discussion of important matters. Finally, it has been suggested that a linkage of the populace in Shakespeare with contemporary political theory and dramatic writing explains partially, but not adequately, a convention which arose from actual social conflict. This conflict, together with its relation to Shakespeare's mob scenes, will be considered in the next chapter.

CHAPTER IV

A New Interpretation

ALTHOUGH Shakespeare writes of preceding centuries and frequently of lands far from England in space and time, the local application is not thereby diminished. In Elizabethan drama overt reference to contemporary events was illegal,[1] but if political scenes in Elizabethan plays were of long ago and far away, applications of them by audiences to current affairs often were not; Shakespeare's contemporaries habitually considered their own political crises in terms of the past. Miss Campbell has shown that warnings against failure to establish the succession and against the ascendancy of royal favorites were often couched in analogies drawn from English historical lore.[2] The publication of Hayward's book on Henry IV was accompanied by official investigation into alleged parallels drawn by the author between abuses in the fourteenth century and abuses under Elizabeth,[3] and Hayward, it was charged, even claimed as an historian's privilege the alteration of historical fact to make more pertinent his message to Englishmen of the 1590's.[4] Mr. Wright has shown that sixteenth-century writers and readers conventionally read history as commentary upon their own times.[5] With these points of view in mind, our task is to dis-

---

[1] See the royal proclamation. Quoted in Gildersleeve, *Government Regulation of the Elizabethan Drama,* pp. 14–15.

[2] "The Use of Historical Patterns in the Reign of Elizabeth," *Huntington Library Quarterly,* I (1938), 135–167.

[3] For a thorough treatment of this see Professor Ray Heffner's article "Shakespeare, Hayward, and Essex," *PMLA,* XLV (1930), 754–780.

[4] *C.S.P. Dom.,* 1598–1601, p. 539.

[5] "The Elizabethan Middle-Class Taste for History," *Journal of Modern His-*

cover, if possible, a contemporary social scene to which
Shakespeare's theme of the populace ran parallel and to determine whether his expression of the theme coincided with
standard practice.

The social tensions which developed by 1642 into organ-
ized rebellion, produced by 1649 a regicide, and led ulti-
mately to the Commonwealth obviously had beginnings in
the sixteenth century; this should be apparent even were
there not confirmatory data. Admittedly, the struggle for
political and ecclesiastical change during the seventeenth century is well known, as are likewise the various factions in that
struggle. But Professor Haller has called for emphasis, hith-
erto slight, upon the early formation of "that state of mind
of which the civil wars, the Puritan Commonwealth, the
Westminister Assembly, and all the pullulating sects, not to
mention *Paradise Lost, Pilgrim's Progress* and much else,
were the eventual expression." [6] Since this underemphasis
has existed in political and ecclesiastical history, it is not surprising that literary history has been unconcerned with such
aspects of the period. For present purposes this period is
roughly 1590–1610, and if during this time there was political ferment which anticipated the later struggle, it may well
be that the political point of view in Shakespeare bears upon
it.

It should be understood at the outset that there will be no
attempt here to relate allusions in plays to specific political
events or persons. Investigation will center, instead, upon
something more general and fundamental: upon an outline
of the times, with emphasis on the political unrest apparent
to theater patrons.

If three Shakespeare plays are to be related to a contem-

---

tory, III (1931), 176–188. See also the same author's *Middle-Class Culture in
Elizabethan England*. The best of all testimonials is that of Heywood, *An
Apology for Actors*.

[6] *The Rise of Puritanism* (New York, Columbia University Press, 1938),
p. 18.

porary political scene, and if there is to be no concern over topical relationship in the ordinary sense of that term, then to what sort of topical connection between the plays and the age may attention be directed? The most promising approach should be to place ourselves so far as we can in the position of Shakespeare's audience: what preconceptions, associations, and prejudices did members of that audience bring to plays which dealt extensively with the populace in terms of English rebels such as Jack Cade, or the Roman citizenry as it is found in *Julius Caesar* and *Coriolanus?*

A successful answer to this question obviously must be derived from popular material accessible to audiences which saw these plays. If emphasis is placed, not upon work of political and religious theorists, but upon public sermons, official propaganda meant for mass consumption, and expressions of opinion by those active in political life, a scheme of things will unfold which is unequivocal, consistent with established patterns of social unrest, and logically related to the beginnings of later political and religious conflict. It will be discovered that the Puritan movement, a moderate one which resulted in a "middle class" revolution, was characterized persistently and quite sensationally as a program of mass rebellion dedicated to leveling of social gradation and even to "Anabaptistical" communism. In addition, it will become apparent that this theme of popular uprising was so habitually expressed in terms of the English Peasants' Revolt, the Cade rising, and Roman civil insurrections that audiences witnessing these events upon the stage would have sensed their application to the Puritan-Anglican issue. This they would have done unconsciously, just as they habitually sensed the bearing of Yorkist-Lancastrian strife upon civil disunity of their own day. The problem of interpreting this is like that which would confront a future literary historian if Kenneth Roberts' historical novel *Oliver Wiswell* had been preceded by a long newspaper campaign which linked the New

Deal with popular "radicalism" during the American revolution.

A few qualifications should precede treatment of Shakespeare's age from such a point of view. The effort here will be to find, not the sole explanation, but one of the main explanations of Elizabethan mob scenes in the theater. There is no suggestion intended, for example, that English traditions operative long before the 1590's are not important factors in the problem; the present chapter is a fragment in the history of the Puritan movement, and it deals, moreover, with Elizabethan public opinion rather than with actual events. Further, there is no intention of ascribing to Shakespeare the habit of writing veiled, complicated or mischievous allegory; to the query "Were Shakespeare's mob scenes so involved and serious as all this?" answer can be made in advance that they were just as uncomplicated and normal as they have been described. They presented entertainingly a very simple idea which, from an entirely conventional point of view, was one widely entertained of Puritanism. It may be added that where the term "Puritan" is used there is no implication that it means generally any one thing; in Elizabethan usage what it meant depended loosely upon who used it as well as upon the context in which it was used; so here. The terms "leveling" or "levelers" used in this discussion are not meant to be Elizabethan terms, nor have they any connection with the later Leveler sect.

The first section of this chapter will present antipopular propaganda roughly contemporaneous with the Cade scenes; it will also be concerned with the emphasis placed during the same period upon the Anabaptists and related phenomena. The second section will repeat this pattern, save that it will cover the period from *Julius Caesar,* another "antidemocratic" play, through *Coriolanus.* The third and final section will deal with the Elizabethan association of dissident politico-religious groups with Jack Straw, Jack Cade, and other traditional popular rebels. It will thus be an attempt to add significance to plays featuring such historical characters.

THE PERIOD OF THE CADE SCENES

In the authorized homily on rebellion, designed to be read regularly "unto the people, that thereby they may . . . learn their duty towards God, their Prince, and their neighbors," it is asserted that the multitude is the backbone of insurrection, that rebellions attempted "by a few ambitious" may "speedily and easily without any great labor" be put down "through the lack of maintenance by any multitudes." These "restless ambitious," because they can prevail against authority in no other way, "do seek the aid and help of the ignorant multitude." [7] The Fourth Part of the Homily contains, moreover, an assurance that "yet were the multitudes of the rebels never so huge and great," and the leaders never so "politic and witty," God has never prospered a rebellion.[8] In *The English Myrror*, "a work safely and necessary to be read of every good subject," George Whetstone writes that a man prone to murder, theft or perjury can be controlled either by the sword of justice or by his own conscience, but not so with "the envious," for "he hideth his conspiracies, until he be strengthened with a multitude, whose fury breaketh forth in the flame of fair cities, and is quenched with the blood of many thousands." [9] Another of Whetstone's tracts on rebellion, a cogent dialogue between "a godly divine," "a discreet gentleman," and "a substantial clothier," is pointed in the title itself at "especially the multitude of ignorant people." In the dialogue Weston the gentleman, in the presence of

[7] *Certaine Sermons Appointed by the Queenes Maiestie, to Be Declared and Read, by All Parsons, Vicars, and Curates, Every Sunday and Holy Day in Their Churches: and by Her Graces Advise Perused and Overseene, for the Better Understanding of the Simple People* (London, 1587), sigs. A2r, Oo5r.

[8] *Ibid.*, Oo1r.

[9] *The English Myrror; a Regard Wherein Al Estates May Behold the Conquests of Envy: Containing the Ruine of Common Weales* (London, 1586), title page and p. 3.

Wilcocks the clothier, exclaims, "Upon God's providences in frustrating the mischievous purpose of Savage the traitor, M. Walker, you have delivered matter of necessary instruction for all subjects, especially the common multitude . . . who are many times tempted to rebellion with allurements of godly and honest appearances." Walker, the divine, also announces later that "the multitude were like unto a barrel that is ready to receive every liquor." [10] Although the traitors discussed in Whetstone's dialogue are not popular rebels in the Straw or Cade tradition, the emphasis throughout is upon aspects of loyalty and disloyalty exhibited by the populace. The populace is commended by Walker, a little inconsistently, for tracking down and wreaking vengeance upon the murderers of Caesar, and it is emphasized that the London commons, similarly, would have "violently intreated every known papist" had the queen been endangered. Whetstone is not an unskillful propagandist. In the present tract the executions of fourteen traitors are taken up, as it were, *seriatim*. After each is described with details, it is used as a point of departure for moralizing, and at the beginning it is made painfully clear that the multitude which flocked to see the executions did not sympathize with the victims. To Whetstone, as well as to the promulgators of the homilies upon rebellion, the populace as a force for good or evil was a very serious matter.[11]

In July, 1591, William Hacket and his two friends Arthington and Coppinger proclaimed their notorious manifesto from a pease cart in Cheapside: Hacket, anointed of the Holy Ghost, was to replace Elizabeth and what are now called "sweeping changes" were to be instituted. The pretensions of this man who thought he was Christ and who, it was said, had once bitten off a schoolmaster's nose and swal-

[10] *The Censure of a Loyall Subiect: upon Certaine Noted Speach and Behaviours, of Those Fourteene Notable Traitors, at the Place of Their Executions, the xx. and xxi. of September Last Past* (London, 1587), sigs. B3ᵛ, D2ᵛ.

[11] Notable in addition to the points of view above is his Coriolanean cynicism at the conclusion of his *Mirour for Magestrates of Cyties . . . a Touchstone for the Time* (London, 1584), pp. 21–22.

lowed it were not looked upon seriously by political realists, but the dubious tumult which followed his Cheapside pronunciamento was magnified into a *cause célèbre*. This will be reviewed later, in connection with the Puritan-Anabaptist equation so popular at the time, but here we may survey it as an indication of contemporary publicity concerning that "beast of many heads," the multitude. Richard Cosin, whose tract covered the affair in repetitious detail, had this to say:

And albeit the common multitude (whom the Disciplinarians brag to be already inflamed with zeal, ready to lend a hundred thousand hands for the advancement of their cause, and by whom they hope and say such reformation must at last be brought in) did better keep themselves out of this action than was expected; yet the danger thereof was as great and, if it had once taken head, would haply as hardly as the other [the Anabaptist rising] have been subdued.[12]

Bancroft, who likewise dramatized the incident in *Daungerous Positions* (1593), declared that "if our said seditious persons had prevailed with the multitude" in their fell design of removing some of the Privy Council, one would have heard no cries of protest from "the brotherhood." Instead, "Oh [some dissenters would have said] the holy discipline, the holy discipline, the holy discipline; what prince or potentate may resist the holy discipline and prosper?" The Hacket affair, with its fancifully alleged threat of mob rule and mob murder of officials on the floor of the Star Chamber itself, takes up the last forty of Bancroft's one hundred and eighty-three pages. Indeed, the material quoted here is from his concluding and decisive chapter.[13]

In an interesting set of manuscript observations published by Burrage, the unknown commentator considers the Martin-

[12] *Conspiracie, for Pretended Reformation: viz. Presbyteriall Discipline; a Treatise Discovering the Late Disignments . . . by William Hacket Yeoman, Edmund Coppinger, and Henry Arthington Gent . . . Also an Answere to the Calumniations of Such as Affirme They Were Mad Men* (London, 1592), p. 85.

[13] *Daungerous Positions and Proceedings, Published and Practised within This Iland of Brytaine, under Pretense of Reformation, and for the Presbiteriall Discipline* (London, 1593), pp. 176, 180.

ist press and some early nonconformists. It is worth noting that his greatest concern is over the virus of dissent having reached the populace.

The factious monsters of the pretended discipline having with these seditious libels (as the forerunners and harbingers of their farther designs) made way in the hearts of the vulgar who ever are apt to entertain matter of novelty especially if it have a show of restraining the authority of their superiors . . .[14]

To judge from the reputation for calm and tolerance of Hooker's *Laws of Ecclesiastical Polity,* one might expect to find in it none of the witch-hunting or the leveling charges against Puritanism which, as we shall see, characterize the work of Bancroft and Cooper. Such an expectation is realized insofar as the mood of Hooker's utterance is concerned, but the warning against the reformers and the populace is much the same. When Hooker attacks the nonconformist position that clergymen should assume apostolic poverty, he does not break into the cry of Bancroft and Cooper that Anabaptist communism would be the next step, but he does suggest with good humor that if the clergy are to live "in meanness of state" as did the Apostles, then the laity should be willing likewise "to be as they were who lived under the Apostles." [15] The secular nature of Puritan discontent is also well understood by Hooker. He charges that it is the natural course of reformers "to impute all faults and corruptions, wherewith the world aboundeth, unto the kind of ecclesiastical government established." By so doing they may gain "with the multitude a name to be virtuous," and the next step is for them to propose change in church government. When this is done, "the nature . . . of the people in the crazedness of their minds, possessed with dislike and discontent at things present, is to imagine that anything . . . would help them; but that most which they least have tried." [16] Hooker, indeed, states

---

[14] "Cotton MS Julius," F VI, fol. 76ᵛ and 77ʳ. Quoted in Burrage, *The Early English Dissenters* (Cambridge, Cambridge University Press, 1912), II, 26.
[15] Preface. Everyman edition, I, 108–109.   [16] *Ibid.,* p. 98.

that one of the means by which the church reformers "both allured and retained so great multitudes" was "a tender compassion which they were thought to take upon the miseries of the common sort." [17] It is very significant, moreover, that Hooker's opening sentence of Book I is: "He that goeth about to persuade a multitude that they are not so well governed as they ought to be, shall never want attentive and favorable hearers . . ." [18]

On the Hacket "uprising" Hooker shows none of the venom of Cosin, but his point of view is scarcely the comic one we shall observe in Thomas Phelippes' letter. He pities Hacket and his adherents as "poor seduced creatures." He compares them to Achitophel and concludes on a very serious note: "If a spark of error . . . falling even where the wood was green" so prevailed, "must not the peril thereof be greater in men whose minds are of themselves as dry fuel, apt beforehand unto tumults, seditions, and broils." [19]

Hooker's position is well expressed toward the end of his discussion of dangers in the Puritan movement, which appears at the end of the Preface.[20] There he calls upon the reformers to reconsider and shift their stand lest crown, nobility, the universities, and the law crumble under it. This was about fifty years before 1642. The only drastic consequence of nonconformist leveling which Hooker does not play up is that of Anabaptist communism. In that respect only is he different, except in dignity and poise, from Bancroft and Cooper.

Thus far reviewed have been some statements of both a popular and official character, roughly contemporary with the Cade scenes and concerned mainly with fear of a subversive populace and mass rebellion. Attention can be given now to a specialized aspect of this, a campaign to impress on the public consciousness a linkage of Elizabethan nonconform-

[17] *Ibid.*, pp. 137–138.　　　　[18] *Ibid.*, p. 148.
[19] *Ibid.*, Dedicatory Epistle to Archbishop Whitgift, II, 4–5.
[20] *Ibid.*, I, 143.

ists with extremist sects: Brownists, the Family of Love, Anabaptists, and others. A large part of this effort called up the floridly publicized Anabaptist horrors on the continent, and thus was an attempt to associate dissent in England with economic and political equalitarianism of the most stringent and recent stamp then available.

Anabaptist militancy in Germany arose about 1525. The so-called Peasants' War, originally a rebellion against feudal exploitation, became dedicated under leadership of the Anabaptist Münzer, to the establishment of a Christian commonwealth with social equality and a community of goods. After defeat at Frankenhausen and the execution of Münzer, the movement crystallized at Münster under Johann Bockholdt, who became known as John of Leyden. After seizure of the town and the deposing of its magistrates, it became the Anabaptist mission not only to hold Münster but also to proceed forth to general influence and conquest. The town was promptly besieged by forces under Francis of Waldeck, its bishop, whom the insurgents had ousted, and was for a year the scene of obstinate resistance and allegedly of anarchic excesses. Doubtless because the Anabaptists actively and candidly refused to separate religious reform from social reform, they were villified by the orthodox with extraordinary zeal during the rest of the sixteenth century. European public opinion was cast against them persistently by inflammatory means until they became the symbols of heinous revolt against established authority. And while the movement never gained a footing in England, the adverse publicity directed there against it was quite as violent as elsewhere. That this official excoriation of the Anabaptists persisted in England throughout the period of Shakespeare and that their communistic tenets were emphasized again and again as a warning against even moderate reform are facts not too generally accepted or understood. An excellent recent account of English sixteenth-century social protest correctly declares that "com-

munism [of the Anabaptist variety] was no jesting matter"
for publicists of the mid-century, but concludes that by 1592
the Anabaptists "remained a by-word, matter for jesting even
among serious minded men." [21] It is true that the jesting was
present, in the sense in which it always accompanies issues
of notorious concern. But it is also true that during Shakespeare's time memory of the Anabaptists was kept alive with
a deadly seriousness and that it was officially used to discredit
Puritan and other nonconformist doctrines which were
alleged to contain the Anabaptist taint. To these points of
view was thus imputed an inescapable drift toward social
leveling, toward an ultimate ascendancy of the "hydra-headed
multitude" so often assaulted satirically upon the stage.

That there existed in England during the late 1580's and
early 1590's an actual tendency toward popular insurrection
and social leveling is, to understate matters, unlikely; the
phenomenon with which we are involved, however, is conservative propaganda and the climate of opinion it sought
to induce. Against opponents of Anglicanism there were
systematically pressed charges recognizable by modern
publicists as name-calling and the device of constant, unflat-
tering association. The campaign of the orthodox which we
shall review is summed up from the nonconformist point of
view in bitterly effective terms. The bishops persecuted their
opponents,

publishing them by their print with privilege [as] Anabaptists, heretics,
schismatics, sectaries, Donatists, Conventiclers; seditious, turbulent,
sparsing abroad through all the land certain Articles of their own de-
vising against them, to bring them into hatred with the whole land.
Whereunto also they have not spared their tongues in their pulpits
where every one of their priests might forge what opinion he list against
them.[22]

[21] Helen White, *Social Criticism in Popular Religious Literature of the Sixteenth Century* (New York, The Macmillan Company, 1944), p. 126.

[22] "A Collection of Certaine Sclaunderous Articles Gyven Out by the Bis-
shops" (1590), A2r and v. MS. quoted in Burrage, *op. cit.*, II, 21.

The Elizabethan-in-the-street would have been clear-headed, indeed, if after submitting to the specimens of public instruction outlined below he had failed to associate the dissenting factions with sweeping popular revolt of the type the Anabaptists had come to symbolize. In 1587 John Bridges wrote of certain nonconformists:

The Anabaptists say that in Christ's and in the Apostles' time there was no Christian magistrate . . . and what [how] does this differ from the assertion of these our learned discoursers: the Church of God was perfect in all her regiment before there was any Christian prince? I do not speak this as though these our learned discoursers did favor of Anabaptistry, or favor Anabaptistry wittingly; God forbid. Howbeit in a heat zeal inconsiderately, they run upon these quicksands.[23]

It is to be assumed that Bridges is endeavoring to be discriminating and fair, but throughout the rest of his tract he alludes with appreciable consistency to Anabaptist doctrines and practices, often enough, indeed, to establish an association of these things with non-Anglican points of view.

That moderates had been consistently linked with extremists was the indignant opinion of Stephen Bredwell. Addressing himself to "the Christian Reader" in *The Rasing of the Foundations of Brownisme,* he rejoices in a "two-fold benefit" from this writing. The first benefit has been that extensive seducing of the "younger and weaker sort" has been stopped thereby; as for the second,

the other benefit is that hereby those impure mouths shall be dashed that heretofore, in their malicious defence of corruptions, have made no conscience to clothe all those, that have dutifully urged the proceeding of our church unto perfection, in one livery with these schismatical spirits; that so they might purchase unto them, both from magistrate and common people, equal hatred and avoidance.[24]

The next few pages will contain many quotations; it is felt that this method of exposition, ordinarily uncongenial, is desirable because by such means a characteristic Eliza-

[23] *A Defence of the Government Established in the Church of Englande for Ecclesiasticall Matters* (London, 1587), p. 134.   [24] Sigs. 4r-v.

bethan attitude upon which the present interpretation depends heavily will appear in its original forcefulness, rather
than in fragments or in unauthoritative paraphrase.
Richard Bancroft, in the opening portion of a Paul's Cross
sermon preached the ninth of February, 1588–89, is not at
pains to minimize conditions.

Of the times in like manner wherein we now live, the Apostle St. Paul
did prophesy that there should be many false prophets; and we do see
his sayings therein to be fulfilled by the number of such prophets as now
remain amongst us: Arians, Donatists, Papists, Libertines, Anabaptists,
the Family of Love, and sundry others (I know not of what opinion) ;
so many sectaries and schismatics as that in very deed divers do revolt
daily to papistry, many are become merely atheists, and the best do stand
in some sort at a gaze.[25]

The device of associating Anabaptists with nonconformists
is pressed further with an account of one who sought to prove
from the prophets that Elizabeth was ordained of God to
be queen of Jerusalem, even, Bancroft adds, "as the Anabaptists long since dreamed of John Bocaldus of Leyden,
whom as Bullinger noteth, they crowned king of Jerusalem." [26]
From here Bancroft expands. In this public utterance he is
characteristically unconcerned about theology; he reminds
his hearers and readers of what is involved in the buttering
of their bread. The "lay factious" are outright levelers,

for say they (as it appeareth in the late admonition to the people of
England, as I conceive by the circumstances there noted) our preachers
ought to conform themselves to the example of Christ and his Apostles.
Their Master had not a house to put his head in. The apostles, their
[the preachers'] predecessors, had neither gold nor silver, possessions,
riches, goods, nor revenues; and why then should they [the clergy] being in gifts and pains inferior unto them, have greater preferments in
the world than they had? If they have a mess of pottage and a canvas

[25] *A Sermon Preached at Paules Crosse the 9. of Februarie, being the first
Sunday in the Parleament, Anno. 1588. Wherein some things are now added,
which then were omitted, either through want of time or default in memorie*
(London, 1588), p. 3.   [26] *Ibid.*, p. 8.

doublet, may it not content them? Surely these advancements which they have do greatly hinder and hurt them.[27]

Lest this be misunderstood as the wry affair of churchmen only, Bancroft hastily converts it into secular terms.

Even as though one should say unto you, my brethren of the poorer sort: these gentlemen and wealthier sort of the laity do greatly abuse you; the children of God, you know, are heirs of the world, and these things which the wicked have they enjoy by usurpation. The earth is the Lord's and the fulness thereof. You have an equal portion with the best in the kingdom of God and will you suffer . . . unequal distribution of worldly benefits? Consider how in the Apostles' time the faithful had all things common. They came and laid their goods at the Apostles' feet and division was thereof made according to every man's necessity. You cannot but groan under the heavy burden which is laid upon you. Your landlords do wring and grind your faces for the maintenance of their pride in apparel, their excess in diet, their unnecessary pleasures, as gaming, keeping of hawks and dogs and such like vanities. They enhance your rents, they take great fines, and do keep you in very unchristian slavery and bondage. Why do you not seek for your better relief to renew the use which was in the Apostles' times? These great possessions, lands, and revenues which the richer sort have in their hands do as you see make them very proud, choke their zeal, hinder them in their virtuous proceedings, and will indeed if order be not taken mar and undo them.[28]

All that is needed is the rhetorical question:

Now dearly beloved, unto you of all sorts, but especially to you of the richest, I pray you tell me how you like this doctrine. Do you think it is true or meet to be taught? No surely it is not. The whole manner thereof is wholly Anabaptistical and tendeth to the destruction and overthrow of all good rule and government. And yet I tell you it may be urged with as great necessity against the laity as the other [the recommendation of poverty] may against the clergy, but indeed neither the one or the other against either of them both truly.[29]

Later in the same sermon Bancroft points out that "Martin in his first book threateneth fists and in his second he wisheth that our parliament . . . would put down lord bishops, and bring in the reformation."[30] And from here,

[27] Ibid., p. 24.   [28] Ibid., pp. 25-26.   [29] Ibid., p. 26.   [30] Ibid., p. 83.

as though it were not only a corollary but also a conscious design of Martinist doctrine, Bancroft declaims upon the path
of equalitarian revolution which he alleges the nonconformists have chosen.

> For how can he [Martin Marprelate] conceive that such a thing
> should be brought to pass (if her majesty do her best to withstand it)
> without a rebellion at the least? . . . Hath not her highness in making
> of laws a negative voice? Is not *lex principis opus?* Hath not every law
> *vim cogentem* of the king?
> I assure you, my brethren, these are desperate points to be stood in.
> And I do verily fear that except good order be taken, and that in time,
> these things will grow to some extremities. For seeing these spirits of
> ours [the Martinists] do follow so exactly and with such hot pursuit
> the outlandish precepts touching the form of their new government, is
> it not to be provided for, lest they fall to outlandish means likewise . . .
> for the erecting and establishing thereof? [31]

A similar diatribe, stressing secular leveling as the goal of
anti-episcopacy and likewise linking the latter with the Anabaptists, is Bishop Cooper's well-known *Admonition*. The
"whole drift," Cooper asserts, is toward a "democracy or
aristocracy,"

> the principles and reasons whereof, if they be made once by experience
> familiar in the minds of the common people, and . . . they have the
> sense and feeling of them, it is greatly to be feared that they will very
> easily transfer the same to the government of the commonweal. For by
> the same reasons they shall be induced to think that they have injury if
> they have not as much to do in civil matters as they have in matters of
> the Church, seeing they also touch their commodity and benefit tempo-
> rally, as the other doth spiritually. . . . The preachers of the gospel in
> Germany, at the beginning were far from meaning to move the people
> to rebel against their governors, but some part of doctrine, undiscreetly
> uttered by divers of them speaking against some abuses, gave a great
> occasion thereof to the grief of all good men . . . until it had cost a
> hundred thousand of them their lives. The looseness and boldness of
> this time in many may justly cause some fear that the like will happen
> hereafter among us. [32]

[31] *Ibid.,* pp. 83–84.
[32] T.C., *An Admonition to the People of England; Wherein Are Answered,*

Cooper is likewise quick to recall the peasants' uprising of 1381 and its rallying slogan of equality in the days of Adam. If such a doctrine be accepted, he writes, "and be allowed as good at this time against the ecclesiastical state,"

it may be you shall hereafter by other instruments than yet are stirring hear the same reason applied to other states also, which yet seem not to be touched, and therefore can be content to wink at this dealing toward bishops and preachers. But when the next house is on fire a wise man will take heed lest the sparks thereof fall into his own. He that is author of all perilous alterations and seeketh to work mischief by them will not attempt all at once, but will practise by little and little and make every former feat that he worketh to be a way and mean to draw on the residue.[33]

Cooper goes beyond the later formula, "No bishop, no king"; he desires a more cogent association to be cherished by his readers : no bishop, no property.

Now, if Christ's doctrine be general to all the faithful, as indeed it is (that being the true interpretation that they would have to be), it must of necessity follow that no true Christian can keep land and possessions nor abide in any wealthy or rich estate: which is the very ground of the Anabaptists' doctrine, as all learned men do know. In so much that all the famous men that in this our age have expounded the Scriptures or written against the Anabaptists, do note that by this interpretation of the speeches of Christ before mentioned, they do ground their community and taking away of propriety and possession of goods, with sundry like other doctrines. We may see therefore, and it is time to take heed of it, how Satan under pretences seeketh to thrust the spirit of the Anabaptists and the grounds of their learning into this Church of England. The inconvenience, then, of this kind of reasoning is either that these sentences of the gospel touch bishops and ministers only and all other are left free, which is a very great absurdity, or else that the same doctrine gathered out of these places, in the same sense that they use, doth belong to all Christians, which [as] with the Anabaptists taketh away all propriety and possessions of lands and goods, and as I have before said, bringeth in a Platonical community.[34]

Not Onely the Slaunderous Untruethes, Reprochefully Uttered by Martin the Libeller, But Also Many Other Crimes by Some of His Broode . . . (London, 1589), pp. 82–84.   [33] *Ibid.*, pp. 157–158.   [34] *Ibid.*, pp. 220–221.

On the immediacy of the social crisis, Bishop Cooper, like certain modern analysts, scatters his ammunition from the bottom to the top of the social scale.

And surely I cannot but fear that the devil is even now in hatching of some notable heresies or some other hid mischiefs which he would bring forth and thrust into the Church of England, and therefore prepareth the way for the same by defacing and discrediting the best learned of the Church that both would and should resist them. This we see already in that peevish faction of the Families of the Love, which have been breeding in this realm the space of these thirty years, and now upon confidence of the disgracing of the state of bishops and other ecclesiastical governors, have put their heads out of the shell, and of late years have showed themselves even in the Prince's Court. The like I might say of the Anabaptists and other sectaries as bad as they.[35]

The hysteria, or at least the attempt to create hysteria, in Cooper's pronouncements is not, of course, that of an obscure Cassandra seeking attention. It is as "official" and as calculated as was Bancroft's Paul's Cross sermon; according to the title page, the tract was "seen and allowed by authority" and "imprinted . . . by the deputies of Christopher Barker, printer to the Queen's most excellent Majesty."

Cooper's attack upon the Martinists called forth retaliation in *Hay Any Worke for Cooper*, 1589. Of special interest here is a repetitive emphasis in the latter document upon one of Cooper's meretricious epigrams into which his whole charge of equalitarian subversion was packed. He had called Martin Marprelate "Martin Mar-prince, Mar-state, Mar-law, Mar-magistrate," and had written that Martin sought to mar "all together, until he bring it to an Anabaptistical equality and community." [36] It is over this rhetorical confection that the Martinist defense swarms with scorn and passion; the catch-phrase is first turned against the users of it: "they who defend this false and bastardly government of arch-bishops and bishops," they who "withstand this true and natural government of the church," by pastors, elders, and deacons—it is they who will prove to be "Mar-prince, Mar-

[35] *Ibid.*, p. 146.   [36] *Ibid.*, p. 36.

state, Mar-law, Mar-magistrate, Mar-commonwealth."
And, "as for Mar-church and Mar-religion, [these] they
have long since proved themselves to be." [37] A page or two
later Martin asserts, "My purpose was, and is, to do good
. . . howsoever some may judge Martin to mar all." [38] And
again, "Take heed you be not carried away with slanders.
Christ's government is neither Mar-prince, Mar-state, Mar-
law, nor Mar-magistrate." [39] Two pages later: "Now, you
wretches (archbishops and lord bishops, I mean), you Mar-
state, Mar-law, Mar-prince . . . Mar-religion!" [40] Another page or two, and the bishops are called enemies to the
state and traitors to God, with the refrain, "Mar-prince,
Mar-law," et cetera, et cetera.[41] And once more, it is the
"Bishops Mar-state" who are accused of usurping civil
authority.[42]

The writer of *Hay Any Worke* is concerned also to correct the impression deliberately created, as we have seen, by
Cooper, Bancroft, and others that all dissenters from
episcopacy belong in a common category of extremism: "For
Martin, good Master Parson, you must understand, doth
account no Brownist to be a Puritan." [43] Nor did the Brownists, for that matter, since we have the testimony of Robert
Browne himself that he had more injury done him "by the
preachers of discipline than by any [of] the bishops." He
asserts that for any single imprisonment by the bishops he
had "been more than thrice imprisoned by the preachers or
their procuring." [44] The Martinists, repudiating the Brownists, were in turn repudiated by the more cautious nonconformists. "I know I am disliked by many which are your [the bish-
ops] enemies, that is, of many you call Puritans. It is their
weakness [that] I am threatened to be hanged by you," writes

[37] *Hay Any Worke for Cooper;* from William Pierce's edition of the Marprelate Tracts (London, 1911), p. 237.
[38] *Ibid.,* p. 239.   [39] *Ibid.,* p. 241.   [40] *Ibid.,* p. 243.
[41] *Ibid.,* p. 249.   [42] *Ibid.,* p. 251.   [43] *Ibid.,* p. 252.
[44] *A New Years Guift;* ed. for the Congregational Historical Society by
Champlin Burrage. Quoted in Pierce, *The Marprelate Tracts,* p. 215n.

the author of *Hay Any Worke for Cooper*.[45] Many Puritans were thus on edge about the free association which connected them with the Martinists. Cartwright, for example, in addressing Burghley found it necessary to disclaim any connection.[46]

Publicizing of the bishops' position apparently had flowered into confusion of all nonconforming sects so far as public opinion was concerned. Martinist disclaiming Brownist, Brownist attacking Puritan, and moderate Puritan rejecting Martinist—what more advantageous tangle could there have been for the forces who were endeavoring to blanket them all under an anarchic program derived from the Anabaptists? Historical parallels to this sort of recrimination and disclaimer should not be hard to draw, and they may be left mercifully to the reader.

Finally, on behalf of the Martinists there was a definitive attempt at clarification which, we may be sure, did not clarify much of anything.

> The government of the church of Christ is no popular government, but is monarchical in regard of our Head, Christ; aristocratical in the eldership; and democratical in the people. Such is the civil government of our kingdom; monarchical in her Majesty's person; aristocratical in the higher house of Parliament, or rather at the Council table; democratical in the body of the Commons of the lower house of Parliament. Therefore, profane T.C. [Cooper], this government seeketh no popularity [popular rule] to be brought into the church; much less intendeth the alteration of the civil State; that is your slander, of which you make an occupation. And I will surely pay you for it.[47]

In addition to this declaration, there were other published disclaimers of leveling doctrine which are excellent evidence of the effectiveness of the bishops' propaganda. The bishops, for example, are accused of dishonestly converting a Puritan program, one of upholding the crown by establishing the

[45] *Op. cit.*, pp. 245–246.
[46] See Strype's Whitgift, App. III, pp. 231–232. From Pierce, *op. cit.*, p. 238.
[47] *Hay Any Worke for Cooper*, pp. 252–253.

kingdom of Christ, into the proposition: "The Puritans, by
their platform of reformation, seek the utter ruin and subver-
sion of Lady Elizabeth, her crown and dignity." [48] And
Henry Barrow sought to answer such declarations as those in
Bancroft's sermon with *A Petition Directed to Her Most
Excellent Maiestie,* probably published in 1590.

Whereas, the adversaries to Reformation do take as a principle that
*whosoever writeth to work a discontentment in the minds of the sub-
jects, do intend a rebellion.* That is a most untrue assertion and sophisti-
cal paralogism. For although rebellion doth grow of discontentment,
yet all discontentment doth not bring forth rebellion; or if the writing
against the state of bishops should move some men to discontentment,
who being discontented should stir up rebellion, yet it doth not follow
that the writers against the bishops were rebels, as this statute doth intend. For the writers must write advisedly and of purpose to stir rebellion. So that if a man write in humble, loyal and dutiful manner, having
no purpose and intent to work rebellion, though rebellion should hereof
ensue, yet could not such a writer without great injustice be drawn
within this statute. For he cannot be a felon that hath not a felonious
intent and purpose.[49]

In this argument, characteristic of those who trust hope-
fully the power of logic to answer gusty libel, there is a
pathetic objective truth which Barrow, the more pathetically,
tries to communicate by having it set in type at least three
times the size of that used throughout the rest of the document. Unfortunately for Barrow, demonstration of the fallacy of the undistributed middle needs more than large print
to be effective against opponents who are striving, not to
win arguments, but to secure property and hierarchy.

In 1590 appeared *A Myrror for Martinists,* a pamphlet
of thirty-four pages filled with indiscriminate linkage of all
dissenting sects, including Catholics. Representative of the
kind of conditioned free association its author sought to
induce is the rhetorical question, "And do we not see that the
same devil employeth still art, learning, ripe wits, and other

[48] *The Just Censure and Reproof of Martin Junior,* in Pierce, *The Marprelate Tracts,* p. 374.   [49] Page 39. Italics are in the original.

good gifts which God hath given unto men, against the truth, to wit, such as are in the Papists, Heretics, Brownists, the Family of Love, Martinists, and all Schismatics . . . ?" [50] Similarly linking the Martinists with extremist sects and with other subversion is the tract, *Martins Months Minde*, which contains a whimsical report of the death and burial of Martin. The second stanza of the last "epitaph" runs:

> O vos Martinistae
> Et vos Brounistae,
> Et Famililovistae,
> Et Anabaptistae,
> Et omnes sectistae,
> Et Machivelistae,
> Et Atheistae,
> Quorum dux fuit iste,
> Lugete singuli [51]

In 1592 appeared Richard Cosin's *Conspiracie for Pretended Reformation*, which, as we have seen, dealt melodramatically with the "rising" of Hacket, Arthington, and Coppinger. That this comic opera disorder was magnified into near-revolution by the official press and pulpit has already been explained. What concerns us here is the way in which Cosin connects the Presbyterian position with Anabaptist leveling. Hacket is pictured as filled "with a most entire, yea burning, desire of reforming (forsooth) the church and commonwealth, by establishing the Presbyterial discipline, which he did imagine would prove like the box of Pandora, for it promiseth cure for all maladies and disorders." [52] Cosin then labors throughout with parallels and analogies between the alleged conspiracy and the still notorious Anabaptist movement with its program for the overthrowing of secular authority.

[50] From "The Preface," sig. A2ᵛ.
[51] Nashe, *Works*, ed. by Grosart (1883–1884), p. 200. See pp. 164–165 for a similar *pot-pourri*. For a statement of the leveling program attributed to the Martinists, see also p. 153.
[52] *Conspiracie for Pretended Reformation*, p. 6.

Were not the treaties of these men also in private houses at nightfasts, and the consultations concerning it at classical conventicles and like assemblies? Did not these likewise shoot at the overthrow of the whole state ecclesiastical and at the displacing of Her Majesty's most honorable council, and that under pretence of Reformation, and to advance the preaching of the Gospel in every congregation throughout this land? Made not these the like complaints of wicked counselors, noblemen and magistrates for keeping out the Discipline, for persecuting sincere preachers, and afflicting God's people like lions and dragons? And do they not pretend this to be a special grievance of theirs that the common people of every congregation may not elect their own minister, that the people are brought under the yoke of the law ceremonial by paying tithes, etc.; and is not the hand and head of Satan, as plainly in this action, to seek the overthrow of sound professors by others of the same profession under pretence of greater sinceritie? Do not these likewise almost appropriate to themselves and their favorites the terms of God's Church, of Christian brethren, and of true and reformed preachers? Is any speech more rife in their mouths than that they will only be tried and judged by God's book and by His Spirit? Do they not tax all other men not so far gone as themselves of loose lives, of anti-Christianism, of hypocrisy, and idolatry, in the mean time never looking at their own treasons, disloyalties, and other vices? Make they not great ostentation of love and fidelity to her Majesty's person and of care of her safety, even when they secretly nourished a fancy of forefeiture of her crown and sought to overrule her by Hacket, their imagined Sovereign King of Europe? Had they not their cabinet preachers, their table-end teachers, their guides of fasts, etc. that teach, pray for, and attend extraordinary callings by visions, dreams, revelations, and enlightenings? Was not Giles Wigginton and some others unto them as Thomas Muncer and Phifer were to the Germans, men of supposed great austerity of life, holiness, favor with God, resoluteness in his cause, singleness, and uprightness of heart? [53]

This is but a sample; Cosin is a devotee of both repetition and pedantry, but his auspicies are as semiofficial as those of Bishop Cooper; Cosin's tract also was published by the "deputies of Christopher Barker," printer to the Queen.

In the *Calendar of State Papers* there is a letter, possibly from Thomas Phelippes to Saint Mains, which discusses from a very different point of view this same aspect of the Hacket,

[53] *Ibid.,* pp. 85–86.

Arthington, and Coppinger incident. The relevant part of it begins, "There be three knaves, one called Coppinger," and the document then recites the well-known Cheapside episode; it continues:

Men talk of it [the Coppinger flurry] and resemble it to that matter of John of Leyden, who took upon himself the kingdom of the Anabaptists, and think this mad fool plotted some such kingdom as these prophets might have assembled; others take them to be mere fanatics, which is very likely, but the enemies to the Puritans take great advantage against them, as these prophets have been great followers of that sort of preachers, and have solicited all those that they knew affected to their sect . . . viz. the Lord Treasurer, Earl of Essex . . . and others who pitied their folly, which is like to cost them their lives; though they be but in the rank of mad men, it is thought the State must be satisfied, especially on the prophet of vengeance because he has said the Queen is not to reign any longer . . . ; meanwhile she is more troubled with it than it is worth, and the Chancellor and Bishop, in the eye of some flattering fools, seem to bear a great burden, for doing their duties to God and the Queen.[54]

Here the Puritan-Anabaptist equation is mentioned as being common talk; there is likewise a shrewd contemporary diagnosis of the propaganda process which is looked upon as deliberate inflation of the Coppinger incident into the proportions of an equalitarian revolt.

Probably in September, 1592, the gentry of Suffolk addressed a communication to the Privy Council, a document which further attests to social uneasiness and a habit of expressing that uneasiness with the Puritan-Anabaptist linkage. "The writers, as magistrates, having a voice," yet forbear to speak their minds, "Lest by their severance in opinion, the law should be rent . . . and so the minds of the people, which are so easily distracted." It is urged that the Council

do not allow the Papists their treacheries, subtleties and heresies, nor the Family of Love, an egg of the same nest, nor the Anabaptists nor Brownists, the overthrowers of church and commonweal. [The Council should] abhor and punish all these. The adversary has cunningly

[54] *C.S.P. Dom.*, 1591–1594, pp. 75–76.

christened them [the petitioners?] with an odious name, not rightly
applied, that they being occupied in defence of their innocency, the
others [above named] might have greater freedom to go about their
hateful treacheries. The name is Puritanism [which the petitioners
detest] as compounded of all the heresies before mentioned.[55]

Confusion confounded—is it any wonder that the term
"Puritan" is used with uneasy reluctance by modern historians?

It will be remembered that the kind of fright expressed
by such propagandists as have been considered culminated
in the statute of 1593 which outlawed certain forms of dissent. D'Ewes presents a meager record of the Parliamentary
debate on that measure, but in his account there is attributed
to Sir Walter Ralegh an estimate of the situation. "I am
sorry for it," Ralegh is described as saying, "I am afraid
there is near twenty thousand of them [Brownists] in England, and when they be gone, who shall maintain their wives
and children?" Although his numerical estimate is exaggerated, Ralegh's appraisal is evidence at least of a climate of
public apprehension. It may be said, moreover, that although
Ralegh does not love a nonconformist and declares Brownists "worthy to be rooted out of a commonwealth," he is
at least articulately aware of the danger to civil rights, such
as they were, of this kind of hysteria.

But what danger may grow to ourselves if this law pass, it were fit to be
considered. For it is to be feared that men not guilty will be included
in it. And that law is hard that taketh life and sendeth into banishment,
where men's intentions shall be judged by a jury and they [the jury]
shall be judges what another means.[56]

Though Ralegh's judicious alarm is restricted to the danger
"to ourselves," it is yet a relief to the modern reader who
may be depressed by certain parallels which history seems to
offer.

[55] *Ibid.,* pp. 275–276.
[56] *A Compleat Journal of the Votes, Speeches, and Debates, both of the House
of Lords and House of Commons* (London, 1693), p. 517.

As a concluding testimonial to the topical zeal with which nonconformists were linked with the Anabaptists, we may hear Nashe; the date here is 1594, which indicates that the Anabaptist scare was nurtured well into the decade. Nor did it stop there, as will be seen later. In *The Unfortunate Traveler* Nashe takes his hero to Münster to be present at the suppression of the Anabaptist rising. The narrative occupies fully ten pages, with liberal moralizing thrown in, much of which connects Anabaptist extremism with the Puritans. This, in fact, is the point of the whole matter, as is shown by Nashe's conclusion of the episode: "How John Leyden died, is that it? He died like a dog; he was hanged and the halter paid for . . . Hear what it is to be Anabaptists, to be Puritans, to be villains . . ." [57]

THE PERIOD FROM *Julius Caesar* TO *Coriolanus*

Arbitrary chronological division of the background material we have reviewed is in one sense unsatisfactory, because the data in question represent an unbroken tradition. In another sense, however, such a chronological separation is valid, because it is necessary to show that substantially the same social conflict was in the air at the time of *Coriolanus,* for example, as during the period of the Cade scenes. It is hoped that the nonliteral reader will see in the somewhat literal sequence an attempt to set forth the unbroken tradition and to provide backgrounds considered applicable at specific times. Accordingly, the pattern of the section just concluded will be followed in this, the second section: first presented will be a series of contemporary manifestations of the fear of popular uprising; this will be followed by material publicizing the Anabaptist scare and relevant phenomena.

We may begin with an excerpt from Shakespeare himself. Although the play from which it is taken was written shortly before *Julius Caesar,* it belongs to this later period, and not

[57] *Works,* ed. by McKerrow, II, 232–241.

to the period of the Cade scenes. In *2 Henry IV* the Earl of
Westmoreland confronts the Archbishop of York and other
rebels.

> Then, my Lord,
> Unto your Grace do I in chief address
> The substance of my speech. If that rebellion
> Came like itself, in base and abject routs,
> Led on by bloody youth, guarded with rags,
> And countenanc'd by boys and beggary,—
> I say, if damned commotion so appear'd
> In his true, native, and most proper shape,
> You, reverend father, and these noble lords
> Had not been here to dress the ugly form
> Of base and bloody insurrection
> With your fair honors.[58]

And in *1 Henry IV* the core of the rebellion, according to
Henry himself, seems to be "poor discontents,"

> Which gape and rub the elbow at the news
> Of hurly-burly innovation.[59]

These Shakespearean prescriptions for the "true, native, and
most proper shape" of civil insurrection emphasize beyond
all else the role of the populace in it. Holinshed, moreover,
furnishes no such material at the point in the story at which
Shakespeare uses it, although there are plenty of data, deriv-
able from the chroniclers, upon popular revolt.

During a session of the Star Chamber in 1599 at which
Essex's Irish disaster was discussed, Cecil made his opinion
on the matter of popular insurrection very clear. Referring
to those "who move the common sort to sedition," he declared: "I have no fear of men of worth; when has England
felt any harm by soldiers or gentlemen or men of worth?
The State has ever found them truest. Some Jack Cade or
Jack Straw and such rascals are those that have endangered
the kingdom." [60] And it is equally significant that one of the

[58] *2 Henry IV, Act IV,* scene 1, ll. 30–41.
[59] *1 Henry IV,* Act V, scene 1, ll. 76–78.
[60] *C.S.P. Dom.*, 1598–1601, p. 352.

interrogatories framed for submission to John Hayward, concerning the latter's account of the reign of Richard II, put the issue thus: "Might he think that this history would not be very dangerous to come amongst the common people?" [61] Moreover, according to D'Ewes' account of the 1601 Parliament, Secretary Cecil spoke again without reservation. At the time of the notorious dispute over monopolies he cautioned the house against public discussion of the controversy, warning them "that the time was never more apt to disorder" and that some disaffected persons "would be glad that all sovereignty were converted into popularity." [62]

London as a focus of popular disorder is exemplified in a proclamation issued closely following the Essex rising. It is recited that

there is at this time dispersed within our city of London and the suburbs thereof a great multitude of base and loose people, such as neither have any certain place of abode, nor any good or lawful cause of business to attend hereabouts, but lie privily in corners and bad houses listening after news and stirs and spreading rumors and tales, being of liklihood ready to lay hold of any occasion to enter into any tumult or disorder, thereby to seek rapine and pillage. And likewise that further numbers of such sort of vagabond people do continually flock and gather to our city and the places confining about the same. [63]

This is perhaps part of the phenomenon publicized in the confession of Essex:

He publicly in his prayer and protestation, as also privately, aggravated the detestation of his offence and especially in the hearing of them that were present at the execution he exaggerated it with four epithets, desiring God to forgive him his *great,* his *bloody,* his *crying,* and his *infectious sin:* which word *infectious* he privately had explained to us, that it was a leprosy that infected far and near. [64]

In Dekker's *Wonderfull Yeare* the "multitudinous spawn" of 1603 is depicted with a morose and morbid imagery.

[61] *Ibid.,* p. 404. [62] D'Ewes, *A Compleat Journal,* p. 653.
[63] Proclamation of Feb. 15, 1600/1601.
[64] *A Declaration of the Practises and Treasons Attempted and Committed by Robert Late Earle of Essex* (London, 1601), sigs. Q4r-v.

Thus far the Prologue, who leaving the stage clear, the fears that are bred in the womb of this altering kingdom do next step up, acting thus:

> The great impostume of the realm was drawn
> Even to a head: the multitudinous spawn
> Was the corruption, which did make it swell
> With hop'd sedition (the burnt seed of hell.)
> Who did expect but ruin, blood, and death,
> To share our kingdom, and divide our breath.
> Religions without religion,
> To let each other blood, confusion
> To be next Queen of England, and this year
> The civil wars of France to be played here
> By Englishmen, ruffians, and pandering slaves,
> That fain would dig up gouty usurer graves:
> At such a time, villains their hopes do honey,
> And rich men look as pale as their white money.[65]

A significant piece of historical distortion also occurs at about this time. At least as early as 1595 Shakespeare, following the chronicles and perhaps Daniel's *Civil Wars,* had shown without heavy emphasis a fickle commons acting as part of the support behind Henry Bolingbroke in his usurpation of the crown.[66] This relationship between Bolingbroke and the populace was entirely traditional; it was echoed, for example, in Drayton's *Englands Heroicall Epistles,* in which Richard's imaginary letter to Queen Isabel contains the bitter but not exaggerated line, "And who but Hereford with the multitudes?" [67] In 1601, however, there appeared an account of the Bishop of Carlisle which describes him as standing between the deposed king and a ravening mob:

When the furious and unstable multitude, not contented that King Richard had resigned his crown to save the head that wore it, and their darling Henry the Fourth seated himself in his royal throne, importuned the Parliament assembled to proceed yet farther against him desiring no doubt that to make all sure his life might be taken from him,

[65] *The Wonderfull Yeare, 1603; Wherein Is Shewed the Picture of London, Lying Sicke of the Plague* (London, 1603), sigs. B2ᵛ–B3ʳ.

[66] In *Richard II.*

[67] *Englands Heroicall Epistles; Newly Enlarged* (London, 1598), sig. F7ᵛ.

this worthy and memorable prelate stepping forth, doubted not to tell them that there was none amongst them meet to give judgment upon so noble a Prince . . .[68]

Holinshed's version, the probable source of this, is remarkably temperate; in it the laconic account runs simply, "request was made by the commons that since King Richard had resigned and was lawfully deposed . . . he might have judgment decreed against him." [69] A "furious and unstable multitude" is no part of the deposition machinery.

The period of *Coriolanus* exhibits similar patterns. With due respect for the claims of those who see in this play a balance—a satire against arrogant aristocracy as well as against a bungling populace; with deference also to the judgment of interpreters who insist that its antipopular speeches are simply in character, *Coriolanus* is still a morose play, and the scurrility leveled at the citizens is felt to be coldly cynical when compared with the vivid horseplay of the Cade scenes, or even with *Julius Caesar*. *Coriolanus* is an historical as well as a dramatic phenomenon and, like the Cade scenes, it deserves to be set in a perspective of events and of public response to them. The unsettled character of this period is, of course, well known but it would be well if a more specific climate of opinion, that of concern over the populace, were established as background.

In 1605 the Venetian secretary in England reported, probably incorrectly, "that a great revolution is on the point of breaking out in this kingdom" and that "the strongest suspicion of responsibility for this falls on the Puritans." [70] Another Venetian envoy reported two years later of the Northampton rising that the revolt was in serious danger of spreading, "thanks to the diverse religions which exist in this king-

---

[68] Francis Godwin, *A Catalogue of the Bishops of England* (London, 1601), p. 540.

[69] Edition of 1586, p. 512. It is true that Holinshed writes, p. 501, of an assemblage of "evil disposed persons" who intended to kill the king, but that is not Godwin's situation, which is one of a "furious" mob intimidating parliament. [70] *C.S.P. Venetian 1603–1607*, p. 219.

dom where the Puritans are expanding continually." The
running account concludes with an opinion that the rising
"has been growing to such an extent that they only require a
leader to make it a formidable and open rebellion." [71]

Coriolanus is contemporaneous with widely felt enclosure
riots of which the Venetian representative, as quoted above,
takes account. A valuable commentary upon this is Robert
Wilkinson's *Sermon Preached at North-Hampton the 21. of
June Last Past . . . upon Occasion of the Late Rebellion
and Riots in Those Parts Committed.* In this dedicatory preface Wilkinson delineates sharply the class conflicts and fear
of popular revolt which his congregation and his London
readers were supposed to sense.

Right Honorable: It is not long since I came forth in a merchant's ship,
and now it is God's providence and your good pleasure that I shall
publish myself in a storm. In the appeasing whereof, since it hath
pleased your Honor to use my service as the word joined with the sword,
or rather as the sword of the Spirit with the sword of justice, I have
discharged myself as indifferently as I could to the cutting down of
offence in all. It is true that we are fallen into tempestuous and troublesome times wherein the excessive covetousness of some hath caused
extreme want to other, and that want not well digested hath rioted to
the hazard of all; yea and by these storms we are cast among the rocks,
even two the most dangerous rocks of estate, oppression of the mighty
and rebellion of the many, by mischief whereof many flourishing kingdoms and countries have miscarried, and so had we in this undoubtedly
had not God by your good endeavors prevented it; and therefore between these two rocks I sail, admonishing in the passage the one sort
—that is, the mighty—that man liveth by bread, but the other sort—
that is, the many—that man liveth not by bread only, to the intent that
they which know the ordinary course of God in preserving nature
might make a conscience of impairing the means of man's preservation,
and they likewise which know that God hath ways to preserve beyond
the means of nature, might learn with Christian wisdom and patience
to temper themselves in want.

Later in his sermon Wilkinson rebukes both the rebels and
the "pasturemen," comments on the relative sinfulness of

[71] *Ibid.,* 1607–1610, pp. 6, 8.

each, and proceeds to the fearful consequences of mass revolt.

. . . and whereas Rehoboam threatened his little finger to be bigger than his father's loins, surely these men's little finger would have been bigger in the end than Rehoboam's loins, for tyranny indeed is heavy in the hands of a king, but it is intolerable in times of commotion when every vile and base companion is a king; and to speak indifferently, I think the sin of these men by many degrees to exceed the other, for pasture-men indeed do horrible mischief but they do it by degrees; first one breaks the law and then another is bold to break it by example; now evils of such passage are more easily prevented, but that which grows by mutinies, being sudden and violent, is less resistible. Pasture-men indeed destroy a few towns but mutineers by civil commotion depopulate whole kingdoms, and that partly by making way to foreign enemies who usually increase their dominions by such advantage, but chiefly by sacking and harrying their own country with their own hands. And let men set what pretence and color they will, yet this hath been from time to time the common proceeding of popular mutinies; first to murmur upon some just cause, as the Israelites did at Moses when he brought them where was neither water to drink nor bread to eat. *Ex.* 15.24 & *Ex.* 16.3. Afterward when they had both to eat and to drink, yet (*Num.* 11) they murmured not for want but for wantonness, *viz.*, for fish and for flesh, for apples and for cowcumbers, etc. Even as many of our malcontents do now, who want not to drink but want to make them daily drunk.[72]

That *Coriolanus,* a play in which the plebeians resolve in the first scene "rather to die than to famish" and in which they later weaken Rome's defenses, should have appeared in such an atmosphere of concern could be more than a coincidence. The acuteness of the enclosure problem, the resultant hunger and deprivation, and the ensuing riots which produced responses such as those of the Venetian envoy and of Wilkinson—all these factors contribute to an attitude of receptivity for such a play. We may let two official declarations complete the picture. It is probably not accidental that about the time *Coriolanus* appeared, a royal proclamation declared,

[72] Wilkinson's sermon was published in 1607. The quoted material is from sigs. A3r-v, F1v-2r.

"It is a thing notorious that many of the meanest sort of our people . . . have presumed lately to assemble themselves riotously in multitudes." [73] This proclamation asserted further that "the glory and strength of all kings consisteth in the multitude of subjects." Nor may it be coincidental that less than a month later another royal proclamation asserted, much in the vein of *Coriolanus*, that "of all other seditions and rebellions none doth bring such infinite waste and desolation upon a kingdom or state as these popular insurrections, which though they do seldom shake or endanger a crown, yet they do bring a heap of calamities upon multitudes of innocent subjects, and chiefly upon the authors and actors themselves." [74]

The last few pages have been devoted to a publicized fear of the populace from the time of *Julius Caesar* and after; we may now consider the more specialized concern shown during the same period over ecclesiastical communism, usually "Anabaptistical."

Middleton's *Family of Love* is a well-made farce-comedy which capitalizes topically upon the extensively alleged proclivities of the sect toward free love and community of goods. It contains a passage of Shakespearean virtuosity.

Gerardine: Who is her accuser?

Dryfat: Her own husband, upon the late discovery of a crew of narrow-ruffed, strait-laced, yet loosebodied dames, with a rout of omnium-gatherums, assembled by the title of the Family of Love: which, master doctor, if they be not punished and suppressed by our club-law, each man's copyhold will become freehold, specialities will turn to generalities, and so from unity to parity, from parity to plurality, and from plurality to universality; their wives, the only ornaments of their houses, and of all their wares, goods, and chattels, the chief moveables, will be made common.

Purge: Most voluble and eloquent proctor! [75]

Henry Ainsworth, in 1604, published a defense of "such true Christians as are commonly (but unjustly) called Brown-

[73] Proclamation of June 28, 1607.   [74] Proclamation of July 24, 1607.
[75] Act V, scene 3.

ists." The brush with which these devout people were tarred appears unmistakably.

Thus have we briefly set down unto your Majesty's view some of the many reasons which the Scriptures do afford for confirmation of the positions which we propounded. Whereby your Highness' wisdom may perceive what weight is in the controversy between this Church of England and us; what arguments do move us to stand in our testimony; what necessity lieth upon us to witness this truth of God in so sundry important doctrines of the Gospel; what cause our adversaries the prelates and clergy of this land have had to pursue us with such manifold and durable calamities; with what equity we have been all manner of ways traduced and divulged to be Donatists, Anabaptists, Brownists, Schismatics, etc.; and whether there be in us the spirit of error, faction, sedition, rebellion, etc.[76]

Ainsworth, as did Barrow before him, attempts to explain away an unjust ascription of leveling made in this case by "the heads and doctors of the University of Oxford." The forthrightness of his disclaimer makes apparent the indiscriminate nature of the charges currently being made.

What must have been designed as a popular version of the kind of attack Ainsworth and his associates underwent appears in Oliver Ormerod's *The Picture of a Puritane; or, a Relation of the Opinions, Qualities, and Practices of the Anabaptists in Germanie, and of the Puritanes in England, Wherein Is firmly Prooved, That the Puritanes Doe Resemble the Anabaptists, in above Fourescore Severall Thinges.* In this tract, the title of which is eloquent, it is carefully explained that although the Anabaptists, like the Puritans, denied under oath that they sought to take authority from the magistrates, "yet shortly after we should have seen it come to pass that they would have been disobedient to all laws of magistrates, if once they had increased to that number that they might have trusted to their own strength." To this charge made by the German of the dialogue, the English-

[76] *An Apologie or Defence of Such True Christians As Are Commonly (but Uniustly) Called Brownists: against Such Imputations As Are Layd upon Them by the Heads and Doctors of the University of Oxford* (1604), p. 80.

man adds that "our Puritans will make as solemn protesta-
tions as any man can do, and by oath deny that which your
Anabaptists did . . . But I marvel they would attempt to
overthrow the magistracy." To which the German makes the
expected reply that such a thing is not at all to be marveled
at.[77]
The topical quality at this time of references to religious
communism is spectacularly attested by Rowlands' *Hell's
Broke Loose,* later to be examined for its insistence upon
parallels between Anabaptists and the English rebels of
1381. It is also borne out by one of William Barlow's sermons, in which he expatiates upon "that very paradox of the
Anabaptists" in seeking charity while at the same time drying
up the source of charity "by inducing a community." [78] Likewise, the 1606 edition of *Albions England* contains a vision
in which Queen Elizabeth, after calling attention to the dis-
paragement of her memory and to the "tyranny of plebal
tongues" in ancient Greece and Rome, concludes,

> Let it suffice. I pardon all, and blessed may proceed
> The Government, of Romery and new Anabaptism freed.

Warner then wakes and finds that this blessing is a figment,
"For when I found I did but dream," he writes, "I could not
then but weep." [79]
In a Paul's Cross sermon of 1608 entitled *The Faithfull
Subject: or Mephiboseth,* William Westerman condemns the
"expectation of the Jews," which he declares, "was not much
unlike to that of the Anabaptists, to pull down magistrates
and governors." Westerman then inveighs against the per-
fectionism of the malcontent "if he look for such an exact
estate so evenly ordered and carried that nothing be
amiss." [80] Reference will be made later to Rowlands' *Martin*

---

[77] All the quoted material is from p. 18.
[78] *Christian Liberty Described in a Sermon Preached in the Collegiate Church
at Westminster, by a Minister of Suffolke* (London, 1606), sig. D1r.
[79] *Albions England* (London, 1606), Book 15, p. 397.
[80] Pages 22–23.

Mark-all (1610), in which the succession of all notorious rogues and vagabonds is traced to such rebels as Cade and Perkin Warbeck. It is significant here that Rowlands, who can be relied upon for a sense of the topical, sees fit to include allusions to ecclesiastical communism. The rogues of London are made to say:

If there be any in our vocation or calling that live disorderly and out of compass, what trade can you name that do not the like. If we sometimes lie with our neighbors' wives, is it not usual elsewhere? (Nay herein by your favor, we do best point out the Family of Love, who do not stick but to have all things in common.) [81]

Thus may be concluded a sequence of topical references to leveling, most of them drawn from the first decade of the seventeenth century. Contemporaneous with these, and also discussed, have been some declarations in which the Anabaptist terror was emphasized. There are doubtless many more; the examples given here are intended to be samples which illustrate by their popular and nonacademic character that the theme of leveling and of primitive communism was in the air.

PROPAGANDISTIC USE OF CADE, STRAW, TYLER, AND
OTHERS; THE ROLE OF HISTORICAL CHRONICLES IN
ANTI-POPULAR PROPAGANDA

Because "antidemocratic" playwriting such as the Cade scenes and *Jack Straw* is a dramatization of chronicle material and because *Julius Caesar* and *Coriolanus* are historical tragedies, it may be rewarding to consider the exploitation during Shakespeare's time of English popular rebels and of other historical figures and materials which involve threat of the populace. Elizabethan historians were frequently propagandistic and more than one item to follow warrants the ap-

---

[81] *Martin Mark-all, Beadle of Bridewell, His Defence and Answere to the Belman of London* (London, 1610), sig. B2r.

plication of Cade, Straw, or the Roman populace to what may be called the Puritan left wing. Indeed, the application is sometimes to what in modern idiom would be called left of center. It may be recalled again that Elizabethan contemporary affairs were habitually expressed and commented upon by the drawing of historical analogies, and in the material below there will be apparent a linkage of nonconformists with English and Roman mob rebellion which is quite as constant as the linkage previously observed between nonconformists and Anabaptists. While the nonconformist-Anabaptist equation showed that Puritans were conventionally depicted as levelers and hence vulnerable to the antileveling satire of mob scenes in plays, the equation of nonconformity with Cade, Straw, Tyler, and the Roman mobs will show a conventional linkage between Puritans and the very characters who were featured most prominently in mass rebellion as it appeared upon the stage. And again it should be recalled that such an interpretation of Elizabethan drama does not depend upon ingenious allegory, but rather upon a free association of nonconformists and stage rebels which was "in the air" as a result of constant publicity.

In Bishop Cooper's authoritative *Admonition* against "Martin the Libeller" (1589), of which notice has already been taken, the linkage between Martinists and the rebels of 1381 is made prominent. According to Cooper, "rebellious subjects in commonweals, when they seek to make odious the princes and governors under whom they live," unjustly impute to them "the cause of such things wherewith they find themselves grieved." And the bishop continues,

So reasoned the rebels in the time of King Richard the Second against the king, against the council and chief nobility of the realm, against the lawyers, and all other states of learning, and therefore had resolution among them to have destroyed and overthrown them all and to have suffered none other to live in this realm with them but the Gray Friars only.

Fifty pages later Cooper makes the same point: the rebels of 1381 were "determined to pull down the state and to dispatch out of the way" the nobility, judges, lawyers, "and all other of any wise or learned calling in the realm." And in this evil program,

was not the way made before, and their states [the privileged classes] brought in hatred of the people as cruel, as covetous, as oppressors of the people, and as enemies of the commonweal, yea, and a countenance made unto the cause and a ground sought out of the Scriptures and word of God to help the matter?

At the beginning, say they, when God had first made the world, all men were alike; there was no principality, there was no bondage, or villeinage; that grew afterwards by violence and cruelty. Therefore, why should we live in this miserable slavery under these proud lords and crafty lawyers, etc.?

Wherefore "it behooveth all faithful Christians" to beware of this guile. If it be allowed now (in 1589) against the ecclesiastical establishment, an entering wedge is thereby driven into the whole social order.[82]

In 1590 the Worshipful Company of Fishmongers presented a pageant [83] honoring the lord mayor and calling up the exploit of William Walworth, once of their fraternity, in killing Jack Straw. Jack himself appears, saying,

> Jack Straw the rebel I present, Wat Tyler was my aide,
> Hob Carter and Tom Miller too, we all were not afraid
> For to deprive our sovereign king, Richard the Second named.

As for the 1381 material here, there is no question that a contemporary application was intended. Prior to the appearance of Straw in the pageant, a speaker riding a unicorn declaims:

> Oh worthy City now rejoice in Christ,
>   for through his grace with peace he hath thee blest,

[82] *An Admonition to the People of England.* The quoted material is from pp. 103, 156, 157.

[83] *The Device of the Pageant; Set Forth by the Worshipfull Companie of the Fishmongers* (London, 1590).

He sends thee still such godly magistrates
as daily seek to keep from thee unrest.

A similar invocation is made later calling upon the lord
mayor to "reform abuses" within the city that his fame may
be eternal and London "still preserved from decay."
The undated *Rythmes against Martin Marre-Prelate* rolls
together not only Martin and Jack Straw; it calls up again
the Anabaptists.

Mark now what things he means to tumble down,
For to this point to look is worth the while;
In one that makes no choice twixt cap and crown,
Cathedral churches he would fain untile,
And snatch by bishops' lands, and catch away
All gain of learning for his prowling prey.

And think you not he will pull down at length
As well the top from tower, as cock from steeple:
And when his head hath gotten some more strength,
To play with prince as now he doth with people:
Yes, he that now saith, Why should bishops be:
Will next cry out, Why kings? the saints are free.

The German boors with clergymen began,
But never left till prince and peers were dead:
Jack Leyden was a holy zealous man,
But ceased not till the crown was on his head.
And Martin's mate Jack Straw would always ring
The clergy's faults, but sought to kill the king.[84]

Bancroft, as we have seen, was not silent on the alleged
parallel between dissenter and Anabaptist; nor does he fail
us when it comes to the analogy of 1381.

A certain writer for reformation having as it seemeth a great dislike of
bishops, compareth the bishop's rochet to a white smock and the Bishop
himself to a porter of the stillyard. This will not dislike some. But
read, I pray you, with patience what he also writeth of noblemen and
gentlemen, for that which he saith toucheth them both alike. Whereof

[84] Page 5. The same stanzas with the same pagination also appeared in *A
Whip for an Ape; or, Martin Displaied.*

came, saith he, this division of such personages from others, seeing all men came of one man and one woman? Was it for their lusty hawking and hunting? For their nimble dicing and cunning carding? For their singing and dancing? For their open bragging and swearing? For their false flyring and flattering? For their subtle pilling and stealing? For their cruel polling and pilling, etc.? No, no; there was no such thing. You would then be glad I am sure to know what thing it was. Indeed the same author doth not conceal it. In effect it is, though it be delivered in better words, viz., that their rebellion and treason against their governors procured them that prerogative with the people. Because, saith he, they revenged and delivered the oppressed people out of the hands of their governors who abused their authority and wickedly, cruelly, and tyrannously ruled over them, the people of a grateful and thankful mind gave them that estimation and honor. We live in a world, you know, that cryeth out: the first institution, the first institution; everything must be brought to the first institution. The words be good if they be well applied. But something was amiss in the priest's application of his text, being such a like saying amongst a multitude of rebels, viz: When Adam digged and Eve span, who was then the gentleman.[85]

On the margin directly opposite the last sentence, which contains the rallying cry of John Ball in 1381, Bancroft provides a note which is illuminating. It has been observed by many that the Cade revolt of Shakespeare's play follows anachronistically certain outlines of the Peasants' Revolt. This could be attributed to intentional synthesis of history for dramatic effect or laid to an influence of the anonymous play *Jack Straw*. If Shakespeare's grasp of the matter was no better than Bancroft's, however, the confusion could be due to ignorance, for the note Bancroft places opposite "When Adam digged" is this: "John Wall, or Ball in the time of Jack Cade's rebellion, in Rich. 2 days." Apparently by 1593 Cade's rising and the Peasants' Revolt could be anachronistically confused even by a well-educated man of Bancroft's position. But although the two rebellions may have become confused with each other, there is little doubt of what

[85] *A Survey of the Pretended Holy Discipline* (London, 1593), pp. 8–9.

they mutually had come to symbolize in the minds of Shakespeare's contemporaries.

The habit of calling up for contemporary purposes the popular rebels of England's past was not present simply during the period of Shakespeare's Cade scenes; its later prominence makes clear the weight and influence of the earlier tradition. In 1599 Secretary Cecil, in a Star Chamber proceeding doubtless meant for public consumption,[86] commented upon "libelous railers who move the common sort to sedition." What he said has already been quoted.[87] It should be recalled, however, that Cecil did not refer abstractly to those who endangered the kingdom; instead, he called up pungently the old association with his remarks upon "some Jack Cade or Jack Straw and such rascals." The topical notoriety of Straw and Cade at this time is likewise borne out by Nashe.

The rebel Jack Cade was the first that devised to put red herrings in cades, and from him they have their name. Now as we call it the swinging of herrings when we cade them, so in a halter was he swung . . . If the text will bear this, we will force it to bear more, but it shall be but the weight of a straw, or the weight of a Jack Straw more, who . . . was the first to put the red herring in straw . . . and the Fisherman upon that Jack strawed him ever after.[88]

In state papers relative to the Essex rebellion there appears "A Memorial about the Insurrection of the Earl of Essex," described as being in Cecil's holograph. In it again appear the rebels of 1381 and Jack Cade: "Wat Tyler cried out for the King and Commons, as you did for the Queen and the Earl of Essex, but soon they commanded the King to meet them at Mile End, and took possession of the Tower . . . Jack Cade termed himself John Amend All." [89]

---

[86] For the propagandistic function of Star Chamber proceedings and utterances see Gladys Jenkins, "Ways and Means in Elizabethan Propaganda," *History* (n.s.), XXVI (1941), 105–114.   [87] See note 60, above.
[88] "The Praise of the Red Herring" (1599), in *Works*, ed. by McKerrow, III, 221–222.   [89] *C.S.P. Dom.* 1598–1601, p. 599.

Analogy between the Essex rebellion and the treason of Wat Tyler appears also in a Paul's Cross sermon preached by William Barlow on March 1, 1600–1601. Barlow gives his auditors the morbid privilege of hearing Essex in the confessional mood of his last hours. After comparing the noble conspirator to Coriolanus, a matter of possible Shakespearean implication,[90] Barlow surges into rhetoric, Biblical lore, and history, in which the climax is again the never-to-be-forgotten events of 1381.

So this his [Essex's] offence and treason, the compound of all the famous rebellions either in God's Book, or our own land, which [he] himself in other words, scatteringly expressed: consisting of Abner's discontentment, of Corah's envy, of Absolom's popularity, of Sheba's defection, of Abimelech's faction. . . . In pretence final, all one with that of Henry, Duke of Lancaster against Richard the Second, removing certain which misled the King. In pretence original, that of Ket's and Tyler's, 'For the King!' as they in your city cried in that [Essex's] insurrection, 'For the Queene, for the Queene!' [91]

Caesar's Dialogue (1601) is a repetitive question-and-answer anatomy of the sin of rebellion which is "not one sin but the sink of all sin." The dialogue is dedicated to "all sound members of that body, whereof her Sacred Majesty is supreme head." In addition to extensive Biblical material, the author, E.N., cites eloquently the familiar English patterns: "So every traitor's offspring may say of their sire, 'Thou hast made me stink among the inhabitants of the land.' What more odious smell to all true English hearts, than the unhappy memory of Cade, Straw, Ket, Perry, and others of like deserts though greater estates." [92]

---

[90] *A Sermon Preached at Paules Crosse, on the First Sunday in Lent; Martij I. 1600* (London, 1601), sigs. C3r-v. ". . . that great natures . . . prove either excellently good, or dangerously wicked: it is spoken by Plato, but applied by Plutarch unto Coriolanus, a gallant young, but a discontented Roman, who might make a fit parallel for the late Earle, if you read his life." Could Shakespeare, later, have been aware of this as a tradition?

[91] *Ibid.*, sigs. D5r-v.

[92] *Caesar's Dialogue; or, A Familiar Communication Containing the First Institution of a Subiect, in Allegiance to His Soveraigne.* Listed under E. Nesbit in the *S.T.C.* Material here is from pp. 14, 52.

A volume called *Strange Histories of Kings, Princes, Dukes, Earles, Lords, Ladies, Knights and Gentlemen,* probably by Deloney, was printed in 1602 and again in 1607. It is composed of ten "cantos" a number of which deal with conspiracy or treason. Significant among the latter as a revelation of subject matter considered topical at the dates of publication is the last: "Canto X. The Rebellion of Wat Tyler and Jack Straw." Here the familiar story, replete with the outrages and fierce cries of the leveling rebels, is told in verse and set to the music of "The Miller Would A-wooing Ride." At the end of it occurs a strange dialogue "between ladies being shepherds on Salisbury plain." The ladies comment chorally and favorably upon the death of Tyler, praise the bravery of Walworth, and are told of the execution of Straw. After hearing of the toll taken by the gallows in 1381, " 'Such ends,' said the ladies, 'send all rebels, and especially the desperate traitors which at this present vexeth the whole state.' " From the rest of the fragment it appears that the traitors "at this present" are the rebels under Audley in 1497. Hence we have the 1381 episode applied topically to a revolt of the fifteenth century and the whole printed as of interest, if not of topical significance, to readers of 1602 and 1607. The devices of association and historical pattern concerning English popular revolt have in this case attained complexity.

Perhaps the star exhibit of this period is what might, with restraint, be called a provocative little volume titled *Hell's Broke Loose,*[93] by Samuel Rowlands. In it is told the old story of the Anabaptists, an account already considered. Important here, however, is the three-fold association made between Anabaptists, the peasant uprising of the days of Richard II, and Hacket's nonconformist "revolt" of the 1590's. In his preface Rowlands calls the Anabaptist rebels "as good commonwealth's men as Jack Straw, Wat Tyler,

[93] London, 1605. Quotations here are from sigs. A2ʳ, A3ʳ⁻ᵛ, B1ᵛ–B2ʳ, C3ᵛ, D2ᵛ, C4ʳ–D2ᵛ.

Tom Miller, John Ball, etc. in the reign of Richard II, and
as sound divines for doctrine as Hacket's disciples that
preached in Cheapside in a peasecart." Then, preliminary to
the narrative poem proper, appears as Prologue none other
than Jack Straw himself.

> I that did act on Smithfield's bloody stage,
> In second Richard's young and tender age:
> And there received from Walworth's fatal hand,
> The stab of Death, which life did countermand:
> Am made a Prologue to the tragedy
> Of Leyden, a Dutch taylor's villainy.
> Not that I ere consorted with that slave,
> My rascal rout in Holenshed you have:
> But that in name, and nature we agree,
> An English traitor I, Dutch rebel he.
> In my consort, I had the priest John Ball;
> Mynter the clerk, unto his share did fall.
> He to have all things common did intend:
> And my rebellion was to such an end.
> Even in a word, we both were like appointed
> To take the sword away from God's anointed:
> And for examples to the world's last day,
> Our traitors' names shall never wear away:
> The fearful paths that he and I have trod,
> Have been accursed in the sight of God.
> Here in this register who ere doth look,
> (Which may be rightly call'd The Bloody Book)
> Shall see how base and rude those villains be
> That do attempt like Leyden; plot like me.
> And how the Devil in whose name they begun,
> Pays them Hell's wages when their work is done:
> "Treason is bloody; blood thereon attends:
> "Traitors are bloody, and have bloody ends.

And the parallel is elaborated later when John of Leyden
links his fellow, Tom Mynter, with the old revolutionary
slogan of 1381.

> Tom Mynter, a mad rogue, our parish-clerk,
> Whose doctrine we with diligence did mark;

He taught on top of mole-hill, bush, and tree,
The traitor's text in England; Parson Ball
Affirming we ought kings apiece to be,
And everything be common unto all:
For when old Adam delved, and Eve span,
Where was my silken velvet gentleman?

Hell's Broke Loose is thus a perfect specimen of what Miss Campbell has called the use of "historical patterns" during Shakespeare's time. While she was not concerned with the present theme of equalitarian revolt, Miss Campbell demonstrated clearly the Elizabethan practice of presenting history in selected episodes which furnished commentary upon contemporary political issues, and the validity of her conception is borne out by extension of it into the area of class conflict. Examples already given and those yet to be examined testify to this, but *Hell's Broke Loose* can be considered the most revealing case in point, as well as one which though neat is representative. Nothing could show better the topical concern over equalitarian pressure; nothing could reveal more clearly the associative process in which Anabaptist communism equals traditional English popular rebellion and both in turn equal contemporary religious nonconformity.

In the writing of *Hell's Broke Loose* Rowlands fell into the conventionally associative patterns just described, but the picture does not end with that. It is apparent that he was reminded immediately by his subject matter of Shakespeare's Cade scenes or, more significantly, of the tradition which the Cade scenes manifest, for in Rowlands and Shakespeare there is a pronounced similarity of material and technique, an emphasis upon farcical Utopianism and preposterous sharing of wealth. Cade knights himself; John of Leyden not only crowns himself "John Leyden, Taylor, King of Munster town," but he also baptizes himself in the following stanza representative of Rowland's clownish capacities.

Well said, art ready? Shall we need Godfather?
Yes: take you Harmon Cromme, or any other:

I have a mind to Knipperdulling rather:
And Tannekin may serve to be Godmother,
Or Knipperdulling joined with Harmon Cromme:
Let it be so: some water; quickly come.

Cade decrees that "the three-hoop'd pot shall have ten
hoops" and that the gutter shall "run nothing but claret wine
this first year of our reign." Rowlands has his rebels "carouse
in glasses that are five foot deep," and John of Leyden decrees,

At every church we'll hang a tavern sign,
And wash our horses' feet in Rhenish wine.

Likewise in the "Twelve Articles of Liberty" given out by
Yoncker Hans in *Hell's Broke Loose* is embodied a program
strongly reminiscent of Cade's objectives: the twelve articles
declare that no one shall stand before magistrates, all men
shall be lawyers, a man may steal a horse so long as he turn
him loose at the end of his journey, spouses may freely change
spouses, tenants need pay no rent, bonds shall be of no effect,
and prisons shall be pulled down. Although it would not be
building too much upon conjecture to infer that Rowlands'
based his satire against ecclesiastical leveling upon Shakespeare's Cade scenes, the point to be made here requires no
such exact relationship; it is sufficient to point out that the
traditions, both of subject matter and technique, which find
expression in the Cade scenes are the ones later brought into
play by Rowlands in attacking nonconformity via an attack
upon the Anabaptists and English peasant rebels, and that
this associative process is one to which Elizabethan readers
and spectators at plays were accustomed.

Another characteristic linkage of English popular rebels
(John Ball in this case) with the Anabaptists is apparent in
Thomas James's *Apologie for John Wickliffe* (1608). Of
Wycliff it is said that "he held the riches and goods of Chris-
tians not to be common, as touching the right, title, and pos-
session (as the Anabaptists now, and a certain Bald priest

in his time did hold) notwithstanding by a Christian charity
they were to be made common, as he teacheth." Later James
re-emphasizes this, observing that he has read in Froissart
"of one John Ball, one of Bal's priests for ought I know,"
who was the chief cause of the rebellion "under the conduct
of Wat Tyler and Jack Straw" which declared an equality
of men and a communion of goods, "which is pure Anabap-
tism." [94]

Two years after this another work by Rowlands was published, a whimsical response to Dekker's *Belman of London*,
called *Martin Mark-all, Beadle of Bridewell*. Here the
author, with a mock devotion to scholarly antiquarianism and
genealogy, purports to trace the succession of all rogues and
vagrants. It is interesting to see what Rowlands, in composing
this *tour de force*, considers a topical stroke; "one John
Mendall (alias Jack Cade)" becomes the original of these
outlaws, and the lineage is followed through such characters
as Perkin Warbeck and a certain Jenkin Cowdiddle down to
the then present.[95]

Exploitation for contemporary purposes of English leaders of popular rebellion persists in tradition long after this
period, and this persistence may be discussed briefly here because it shows how strong the original impulse must have
been. In more recent and more republican times the men of
1381 are celebrated sympathetically in the manner of South-
ey's *Wat Tyler* and William Morris's *A Dream of John Ball*.
A glance at the seventeenth and eighteenth centuries, however, will show the older tradition still active. In the critical
year 1642 a satirical pamphlet appeared, "published by Antibrownistus Puritanomastix" and called *The Speech of a
Warden to the Fellowes of His Company: Touching the*

[94] *An Apologie for Iohn Wickliffe, Showing His Conformitie with the Now
Church of England* (Oxford, 1608), pp. 37, 65.
[95] *Martin Mark-all, Beadle of Bridewell; His Defence and Answere to the
Belman of London, Discovering the Long Concealed Originall and Regiment
of Rogues . . . Gathered Out of the Chronicle of Crack Ropes, and (As They
Terme It) the Legend of Lossels* (London, 1610), sigs. F1ᵛ–H1ᵛ.

*Great Affaires of the Kingdome . . . and Doubtlesse Is
Such a Speech As Was Never Spoken by Any Warden.* The
warden in his oration has difficulty with words; after efforts
with "Liturgy" he comes to "Militia." This "Militia," he
asseverates, "is Colonel of all the hard words that ever came
into the city since the valiant conquest of *Wat Tyler* and *Jack
Straw,* performed by a citizen and predecessor of ours." [96]
And in his meaning the "predecessor of ours" is, of course, a
predecessor of the Puritans.

Another interesting adaptation of the 1381 theme to
changing topical conditions appears in play form in 1730.
*Wat Tyler and Jack Straw: or The Mob Reformers; a
Dramaticke Entertainment* [97] is described on the title page
as having been "perform'd at Pinkethman's and Gifford's
Great Theatrical Booth in Bartholomew Fair." There are
here some characteristic and remarkable eighteenth-century
accretions: Sir William Walworth is provided with a son who
is in love with Aurelia, daughter to Suffolk. There are additions of Goody Tyler (Wat's mother) and Suky Tyler (his
daughter) whose farcical passion for Jack Straw, her be-
trothed, balances the relationship between Aurelia and the
younger Walworth. Both girls in disguise follow their men
into battle and disclose themselves at critical moments,
Aurelia to urge Walworth on to glory, and Suky to beg for
amorous violence before it is too late. The play is a farce, with
no uncertainty, however, concerning the dignity of its aristocratic characters and the clarity of its political message. As
the action closes, the elder Walworth having been honored,
Aurelia and the younger Walworth united, Suky separated
from Straw by inexorable justice, and the rank and file of the
rebels pardoned, King Richard announces chorally,

> Succeeding ages shall with pleasure read
> The bold relation of th' immortal deed
> [the killing of Tyler]

[96] Sig. A2.   [97] London, 1730.

'Till in the happy years of George's reign,
Another race shall grace our isle again,
Loyal as this, undaunted, and as free,
Great, and not proud—yet proud of liberty.
United Europe shall be lull'd in peace,
And only then the loyal wonder cease.

Jack Straw was apparently as adaptable for topical dramatic purposes in 1730 as he was in the 1590's. The persistence of the theme as late as the eighteenth century is an indication of its earlier vitality in the period with which we are concerned.

Because plays which featured Cade, Straw, Tyler, and others would have been recognized as employing chronicle materials, it is interesting to observe what writers against popular sedition had to say of the function of chronicles. By this means historical plays involving popular rebellion may be set in the perspective of a more general program for molding public opinion. In the official homily against rebellion, already noted as being designed with the populace in mind, congregations who wish to know the consequences of revolt are urged to "turn over and read the histories of all nations, look over the Chronicles of our own country . . ." [98] Similarly advised is the reader of Compton's *Short Declaration of the Ende of Traytors* (1587): What happened to "Doctor Makerell and others of the chief of that rebellious company? . . . Look into Grafton's abridgment of Chronicles, and there you shall see it." What occurred in the reign of Edward I "when a great number rebelled in the west parts of this realm?" "Look into the said abridgment." What of Wyatt's rebellion? "Look into the same book and there it is plainly set down." [99] In *Histriomastix* there is a mob scene beginning with the stage direction *"A Noise within crying, 'Liberty, liberty.' Enter a sort of Russetings and Mechanicals, Fury*

[98] *The Fourth Part of the Homilie against Wilfull Rebellion*, sig. Oo1ʳ.
[99] *A Short Declaration of the Ende of Traytors, and False Conspirators Against the State* (London, 1587), sig. B4ᵛ.

leading them, and crying confusedly." The leader shouts in the manner of Dogberry, "Stay my Masters, we have not insulted yet . . . !" During the ensuing "insultation," another member of the mob cries, "we'll pluck down all the noble houses in the land, e're we have done." To which the first replies, "It were a most noble service, and most worthy of the Chronicle." [100] In one of his anti-Martinist pamphlets, *Pasquils Returne to England,* Nashe declares that "the Chronicles of England and the daily enclosures of commons in this land teach us sufficiently how inclinable the simpler sort of the people are to routs, riots, commotions, insurrections, and plain rebellions when they grow brain sick. . . . They need no Travers or Martin to increase their giddiness." [101]

The introduction to Stow's *Annales* designates as a primary function of "Chronicles and Histories" the "discouragement of unnatural subjects from wicked treasons, pernicious rebellions, and damnable doctrines." [102] William Covell recites in *Polimanteia* (1595) a litany of rebellion in all lands, ending with "the intolerable boldness in Kent by Jack Straw and his accomplices." Summing this up, Covell declares, "These things and many such, howsoever smoothed over with a fair show, have been committed by unnatural subjects since Her Majesty's reign, that our very enemies for the state of our country could by no means possible have deserved worse." And on the margin opposite this summation Covell repeats the well-worn advice, "Read the chronicles." [103] In some elegiac stanzas on the death of Elizabeth is the following:

> All those that please the Chronicles to read,
> shall see how God did keep her with his power:
> And by the hand (as 'twere) her grace did lead,
> even from her birth day, to her latest hour:

[100] *Histriomastix,* Act 5.
[101] *Works,* ed. by Grosart (1883–1884), I, 107.
[102] From the preface, "To the gentle Reader," edition of 1592.
[103] The Covell quotations here are from sigs. Cc3^r, Cc4^v.

And many traitorous acts against her grace,
Did bring to light, and utterly deface.[104]

Many, of course, are aware that Heywood wrote in his
Apology for Actors that "plays are writ with this aim . . .
to teach the subjects obedience to their King, to show the
people the untimely ends of such as have moved tumults, commotions, and insurrections." [105] It is very important, however, to observe the means by which Heywood considered
this to be accomplished; "Players," he declared, "have . . .
instructed such as cannot read in the discovery of all our
English Chronicles." [106] When John Green replied in the
Refutation of the Apology for Actors, that "these that know
the Histories . . . are ever ashamed when they have heard
what lies the players insert amongst them," [107] one wonders
whether among other things he was thinking of the Cade
scenes, certainly libelous history when compared to the account of Holinshed.

Finally, on the specialized relationship of the chronicles,
and therefore of chronicle plays, to the problem of revolt it
is important to take note of a special type of history which
was a compendium of rebellion, a methodically concentrated
series of object lessons produced by squeezing the larger and
more general chronicles dry of their episodes of sedition and
subversion. Examples of these are Anthony Munday's
Watch-woord to Englande (1584), Compton's *Short Declaration of the Ende of Traytors* (1587), the tenth book of
Albions England (1597), and Book II, chapters 2 to 5, of
Thomas Beard's *The Theatre of God's Judgements* (1597).
To this list, with all respect due to the difference in quality,
one might add Shakespeare's cycle of history plays, as well
as certain of the tragedies.

Supplementing this evidence, which indicates the propa-

104 *The Poores Lamentation for the Death of Our Late Dread Soveraigne*
(London, 1603), sig. B1ᵛ.
105 *An Apology for Actors* (London, 1612), sig. F3ᵛ.   106 *Ibid.,* sig. F3ʳ.
107 *A Refutation of the Apology for Actors* (London, 1615), p. 42.

gandist function of the chronicles, are some outright statements of topical policy in the writing and reading of history.
In Munday's *Watch-woord*, previously noted as a chronicle
of rebellion, there appears on the title page a warning "to
beware of traitors and treacherous practises which have been
the overthrow of many famous kingdoms and commonweals." Nor is topical interpretation of history scorned by
William Covell.

The truth hereof is apparently known, both by ancient histories and of
later time, not only within these small dominions hemmed with the
narrow seas, but in populous and large Italy, within the walls of proud,
stately and commanding Rome, where the often secessions of the common people to the Mount Aventin may plainly testify that, malcon-
tented, they pretended a reformation of the rich nobility. So that the
horrible, strange, and detested practices of our time, which some most
irreligiously have plotted to obtain their purpose (being nothing in
truth but an overflowing ambition, and an insatiable desire to rule)
have been smoothed over with the fine terms of a common good, of the
freedom of the people, of justice, of religion, of reformation, and such
like, things only mentioned in name and no further intended than in a
bare show. Thus dealt they that sought to alter the Roman Empire by
lighting the torch of civil dissension, pretending the more easily to win
the people, to free them from subsidies and oppression which then
seemed by their governors to lie upon them, making a show to the common sort that they tendered their case in so great a measure . . .[108]

There is little doubt that Covell or his readers would have
interpreted *Julius Caesar* or *Coriolanus* topically. The same
is true of Fulbecke's *Historicall Collection of the Continuall
Factions, Tumults, and Massacres of the Romans*. Fulbecke
writes in his preface that "the use of this history is threefold;
first, the revealing of the mischiefs of discord and civil dissension . . . Secondly, the opening of the cause hereof
which is nothing else but ambition . . . Thirdly, the declaring of the remedy." This remedy, according to the euphuistic
Fulbecke, is to be compounded "by living well, not by lurking
well: by conversing in the light of the common weal with

[108] *Polimanteia*, sigs. Cc1ᵛ-2ᵛ.

equals, not by complotting in dark conventicles against superiors." [109] Such a probable association of Roman rebellion
with separatist "conventicles" may seem far-fetched to us,
but it appears to have been almost an automatic linkage for
writers such as Covell and Fulbecke.

Another title-page statement of topical purpose in chroni-
cling rebellion is found in Richard Johnson's *Lanterne-Light
for Loyall Subjects* (1603). Johnson's catalogue of revolt,
Biblical, Roman and English, is prominently declared to be
"a matter rightly agreeing with this time of danger, where
wicked persons have desired our public sorrow, and the ruin
of this realm of England." A final declaration of overt topical
motive is to be read in *Hell's Broke Loose*. We have observed Rowland's indiscriminate likening of his Anabaptists
to Straw, Tyler, and Ball, of 1381, and to Hacket's disciples
of 1591. The preface in which this is done contains a formulation of the agelessness of the theme. "Infinite are the examples . . . out of the registers of foregone ages . . . how
the people, affecting novelties and innovations, have con-
curred from time to time with the plotters' endeavors. Histories are full of their memories. Most rebellions do pretend
religion for themselves." [110]

The same principle is again declaimed in Rowlands' "Argument."

> For all the sins that Hell's vast gulf contains,
> In every age, and every kingdom reigns:
> Murder, and treason, false disloyal plots,
> Sedition, heresy, and roguish knots:
> Of trait'rous rebels; some of highest place,
> And some of meanest sort, most rascal base:
> Of which degree, behold a cursed crew,
> Such as Hell's mouth into the world did spew. [111]

We are now, perhaps, in a position to imagine an audience
of Shakespeare's time as it witnessed the Cade scenes, *Julius
Caesar,* or *Coriolanus.* On the stage a notorious rebel of

---

[109] London, 1601. From the Preface.
[110] From the preface, "To the Reader," sigs. A1r-v.   [111] Sig. A4r.

English history incites his blundering followers to level all distinctions of property and of caste. Or a Roman mob, fickle and discordant, by asserting its democratic influence makes of the political scene a shambles or a madhouse. Lively drama and astringent conservative satire—these the audience enjoys with abandon and certainly with none of the analysis which has characterized these pages. We may even grant the dubious claim of sentimentalists that not a thought is troubling the good-humored heads of these playgoers. Something, however, has taken its toll long before they have entered the theater. They have heard it preached and have heard it said unceasingly that the muster of nonconformists is growing steadily, that the inescapable goal of nonconformity is wholesale leveling, and that the true ancestors and equals of troublemakers in their midst are English peasant rebels and the unstable Roman plebs. They have been told in sermons and have heard it rhymed in season and out that Jack Cade, Jack Straw, the Roman mobs, and the Anabaptists are all one and that together or individually they spell out the Puritan, "Presbyterial," or Brownists disciplines, all of which are to be lumped together. Members of this audience, moreover, scarcely have the quaint attitude of modern theory (but not of modern practice) that entertainment is separate from moral or political instruction, nor do they conceive the function of history or historical drama in any such amoral and bifurcated fashion. They read history or see it on the stage; they enjoy its color, conflict, and pageantry; and they react with equal zest to its lesson, which is not addressed to antiquarians, but by parable and parallel to the living moment— to the uncertain state of their own time. Shakespeare's audiences saw in his main historical theme of Yorkist-Lancastrian conflict a solemn political lesson applicable to their day, and they did so because they had been "conditioned" to such an interpretation.[112] In similar fashion they would have been

[112] The recent studies of Miss Campbell, *op. cit.*, and Mr. Tillyard, *op. cit.*, are recommended to any reader to whom this is not now a commonplace. See note 50, Chapter III.

prone to view his mob scenes and plays as engaging commentary upon dangerous mass tensions to be found in their own midst, for their conditioning in that direction had been equally thorough.

The ironic qualification remains. We have been considering audience responses as though they were unanimous. But some of Shakespeare's spectators doubtless were irritated by implications of the mob scenes and large numbers who conscientiously avoided the theater were oblivious of them. These factions triumphed in 1642, and although there were unpleasant souls among them, our debt to the Puritans is as incalculable as our debt to Shakespeare.

CHAPTER V

Some Other Dramatists and Poets

IT IS NOT proposed to render here a minute survey of the mob theme in Elizabethan literature. No study of the theme in Shakespeare would be adequate, however, if there were failure to compare his performance with that of certain other dramatists and poets who were representative both of the Elizabethan conservative norm and of departure from it. From the rather extensive data of Chapter IV it is clear that Shakespeare's attack upon the common mass for excesses of leveling, bungling, and instability was typical of a conservative position which sought to discredit both moderate and extreme dissent. It is both well known and unsurprising that other dramatists attacked the populace, and a demonstration that Shakespeare was not the only playwright who did so would be rather pointless. But if a thorough sampling of Shakespeare's literary contemporaries should raise a presumption that there were attitudes other than the one he represented, the result will be far from pointless. From the description which follows of literary practices which were both conventional and unconventional, or better still from a reading of the literature described, some fundamental variations as well as similarities in political points of view will be apparent.

THE LIFE AND DEATH OF JACK STRAW

Comparison may begin with this anonymous play. In the opening lines a tax collector presents his demands and is challenged thus by the title character:

> . . . thou gettest no more of me.
> For I am sure thy office doth not arm thee with such
>   authority,
> Thus to abuse the poor people of the country.

As the collector attempts to search Straw's daughter, because he does not believe she is under fourteen and therefore "goes clear," Straw kills him. Then enter Ball, Tyler, Nobs, and Tom Miller; rebellion is decided upon, and Ball proclaims a manifesto.

> But when Adam delved and Eve span
> Who was then a gentleman?
> Brethren, brethren, it were better to have this
>   community,
> Than to have this difference in degrees.

The rebel priest then calls to mind the ancient days in which there was neither property nor usury. He concludes:

> The rich have all, the poor live in misery;
> But follow the counsel of John Ball,
> I promise you I love ye all,
> And make division equally,
> Of each man's goods indifferently,
> And rightly may you follow arms
> To rid you from these civil harms.

Following this, aristocratic characters take the stage. The Archbishop speaks of the rebels as "the multitude, a beast of many heads" and declares that this beast deems the last benevolence granted by Parliament to the king,

> A matter more required for private good
> Than help or benefit of common weal.

Wherein the Archbishop's conscience bears witness "how much they [the multitude] wrong the better sort." A note of social consciousness is now contributed by the "Secretary," who grants diffidently that the profit of the king is the profit of the land.

> Yet give me leave in reverence of the cause,
> To speak my mind touching this question:
> When such as we do see the people's hearts
> Expressed as far as time will give them leave,
> With heartiness of their benevolence,
> Methinks it were for others' happiness
> That hearts and purses should together go.

But "misdeem not" this speech, he hastily adds; he is well aware that the noble and the slave live but for the commonweal, and that the commonweal is the king's. There is no reply to this uncertain liberalism, for a messenger arrives telling of the gathering storm.

Next occurs a scene, similar to Shakespeare's Cade episode, in which the rebels plan grand strategy. It is "Captain" Straw this and "Captain" Carter that, all in the familiar satirical vein. In Act II, moreover, the rebels are shown stealing from each other, and they are reported to "have spoiled all Southwark, let out the prisoners, broke up the Marshalsea and the King's Bench, and made great havoc in the borough here." As this is announced Morton, who is an unwilling gentleman-hostage and messenger of the rebels, breaks in with choral commentary as climactically timed as any in Shakespeare.

> What mean these wretched miscreants
> To make a spoil of their own countrymen:
> Unnatural rebels, what so e'r,
> By foreign foes may seem no whit so strange,
> As Englishmen to trouble England thus.
> Well may I term it incest to the land,
> Like that foul lawless force and violence
> Which Cyneris did offer to his child.

What is to be the "end of this attempt" but a glutting of the land with blood?

A Fleming is now dragged in and led off to execution by the rebels when he fails to pass their test, which is the pronunciation of "bread and cheese" without foreign accent.

Act III brings together the rebels and the young King Richard. When Straw is asked to state his demands, he asserts simply, "We will have wealth and liberty," to which cry all, "Wealth and liberty!" The young king asks them if they demand more "than to be free," and they cry in reiteration, "Wealth and liberty!" The king promises general pardon which the Essex men accept, but Straw pronounces,

> Content, let them go suck their mams at home,
> I came for spoil and spoil I'll have.

The play is climaxed with the stabbing of Straw by William Walworth, the mayor of London, and tapers off with a reading to the rebels of the king's pardon, which is preceded by a formal heading in large type.

THE KING'S PARDON DELIVERED BY
SIR JOHN MORTON TO THE REBELS

The typography thus indicates a stiff and didactic quality intended for choral recitation:

My friends and unhappy countrymen. . . . I am sent unto you . . . to give you to understand that, notwithstanding this violence which you have offered to yourselves in running furiously into the danger of the law, as mad and frantic men upon an edged sword: yet notwithstanding, I say, that you have gathered rods to scourge your own selves, following desperately your lewd and misgoverned heads which have haled you on to this wretched and shameful end which is now imminent over you all, that must in strangling cords die like dogs . . . because you would not live like men: But far unlike yourselves, unlike Englishmen, degenerate from your natural obedience and nature of your country, that by kind bringeth forth none such, or at least brooketh none such, but spits them out for bastards and recreants: notwithstanding, I say . . . yet it hath pleased the king of his accustomed goodness to give you your lives.

Except, of course, the "accursed and seditious priest," John Ball, and Wat Tyler. Tyler is now pointedly described as an "example to all Englishmen hereafter." Walworth is knighted.

SPENSER'S EPISODE OF THE GIANT AND THE SCALES

In this episode of *Faerie Queene,* Book V,[1] Artegall, the personification of justice, confronts a giant who is making harangue to a multitude of people; the giant stands upon a rock and holds before the crowd "a huge great pair of balance," with which, he boasts,

> That all the world he would weigh equally,
> If ought he had the same to counterpoise.
> For want whereof he weighed vanity,
> And filled his balance full of idle toys:
> Yet was admired much of fools, women, and boys.

According to the giant, the four elements have encroached upon each other and have deviated from their original balance; "realms and nations," moreover, have run awry. This departure from original dispensation and adjustment, the giant proposes to correct.

> All which he undertook for to repair,
> In sort as they were formed anciently;
> And all things would reduce unto equality.
> Therefore the vulgar did about him flock,
> And cluster thick unto his leasings vain,
> Like foolish flies about an honey crock,
> In hope by him great benefit to gain,
> And uncontrolled freedom to obtain.

Artegall challenges the giant with the principle of immutable "degree" so familiar to readers of Shakespeare. He also tells him that even were benefits to be redistributed by weighing things anew,

> We are not sure they would so long remain:
> All change is perilous, and all chance unsound.

And after rebuking the giant with cold orthodoxy, Artegall shoulders him from the rock into the sea, where he is drowned. Talus then scatters with his flail the "lawless multitude," which scurries for refuge into "holes and bushes."

[1] The quoted material here is from Book V, Canto 2, stanzas 30–36.

A standard interpretation of the allegory here is that the episode is an arraignment of the Anabaptists and their well-known communistic tenets. In reaching this conclusion the late Professor Padelford,[2] after querying what sect in Spenser's day represented the equalitarian and communistic leanings which the giant voices, asserted that the Anabaptists did so notoriously. This is true beyond a doubt, but in view of the continual ascription of leveling to English nonconformists of the 1590's and the inveterate linkage of them with Anabaptist extremists, it is more likely that the flail of Talus is here directed against native English "radicalism." From the passage quoted, moreover, it is plain that the giant wants things restored to their original equality, a return to "the first institution" emphasized so violently by Bancroft and others as the basic aim of nonconformists which placed them on a footing with the Anabaptists.

There is one difficulty with this more immediate application of the episode: Spenser is thought to have been a Puritan of sorts, and we have seen that orthodox propaganda had stigmatized all nonconformists with the leveling taint. If so, is it then likely that Spenser intended to join Bancroft, Cooper, and others in a vindictive attribution of leveling to the Puritan faction?

It may be answered that the evidence for Spenser's Puritanism establishes little more than his dislike of materialism and corruption among the clergy and his corresponding sympathy for such a tolerant cleric as Grindal. It is also possible that by the time Book V of *The Faerie Queene* was written Spenser had become more conservative than he was in the days of the *Calender;* he had entered government service and was probably not immune to the influence of increasing crisis and increasing anti-Puritan publicity. Mr. J. B. Fletcher believes, however, that Spenser carried Puritan beliefs over into the later period of *The Faerie Queene;* [3] he asserts that

---

2 "Spenser's Arraignment of the Anabaptists," *JEGP*, XII (1913), 434-448.
3 "The Puritan Argument in Spenser," *PMLA*, LVIII (1943), 634-648.

there "is a reasonable antecedent probability, in absence of evidence to the contrary, that Spenser would not change his religious convictions." There is, of course, no antecedent probability of any kind that a man will cling to his youthful nonconformity. In any event, Spenser's episode of the giant and the scales exhibits the conventional point of view toward economic and class leveling, a point of view which at the time was being expressed indiscriminately with reference to the anti-Anglican position.

THE PLAY OF SIR THOMAS MORE

The "Ill May Day" episode [4] of *The Play of Sir Thomas More* follows closely the standard pattern of mob scenes in Elizabethan plays. The first scene exhibits the citizenry in a state of brewing discontent arising from economic competition with aliens who have settled in London. At the end of the scene a statement of grievances appears in a bill of complaint which accuses the foreigners of responsibility for the beggary of native craftsmen. The next scene (cf. the sequence in *Jack Straw*) characteristically views the incipient rising from the other side, that of constituted authority, with officialdom in a state of apprehension as reports are brought in of growing disorders. These reports occasion rhetorical comment like Shrewsbury's:

> I tell ye true, that in these dangerous times
> I do not like this frowning vulgar brow.

The next scene returns to the citizens, now about to riot, who send up a repeated cry for burning the houses of the outlanders, and in Scene 5 it is announced that the rioters have delivered the prisoners from Newgate.

Now comes the characteristic encounter of the mob with the forces of order. Sir Thomas More and other officials enter amidst tumult, and an episode obviously in the pattern

[4] The "Ill May Day" scenes are edited critically by W. W. Greg. Publications of the Malone Society (1911).

of *Julius Caesar* ensues; it even begins with Surrey's "Friends, masters, countrymen," interrupted by "Peace! Ho! Peace," and continues with Shrewsbury's "My masters, countrymen." To which the crowd shouts, "The noble earl of Shrewsbury, let's hear him" and "We'll hear the Earl of Surrey." True, there is nothing here about the lending of ears, but anyone familiar with the episode of Brutus' and Antony's orations will recognize the parallels both of situation and of verbal usage. R. W. Chambers believed that these similarities are to be included in the evidence that Shakespeare himself wrote the scene.[5]

The delivery of More's speech follows; it is the standard pronouncement against public disorder and is doubly characteristic of contemporary mob scenes in its timing, for it arises dramatically as a climax and summation in the fashion of the Prince's denunciation of the rioters in *Romeo and Juliet* or of Menenius' fable of the belly and the members in *Coriolanus*.

Certainly no more tractable, reasonable, and sweet-tempered people ever assembled in an Elizabethan mob scene than those gathered here to attend More's words. They respond with intuitive and immediate respect to his request that they behave toward foreigners as they would have foreigners behave toward them, and they are instantly impressed by More's observations that the peace of England is their dearest possession. After some hundred lines of More's speech, interpolated with their own shouts of agreement, they have gently laid down their arms on the promise of pardon. Nor in the next scene, in which the principal offenders are about to be hanged, is there any cessation of this love-feast between commoner and magistrate. All prepare for execution with chivalry toward each other, with warm words on the reasonableness of their fate, and with a modest insouciance which would have been envied by condemned aristocrats during the

---

[5] *Shakespeare's Hand in the Play of Sir Thomas More*, p. 164.

Reign of Terror. Needless to say, the pardon arrives in proper order and in time; but such an atmosphere of good will has grown up that one feels sorry for the well-intentioned sheriff who is rebuked for having almost allowed the executions to proceed on schedule. If Shakespeare's hand in the Ill May Day scenes is ever conclusively established, certain critics will no longer be under the strain of trying to demonstrate that mobs of the Cade scenes and the Roman plays are mellowly conceived. They will have a new mob in the Shakespeare canon which is everything a well-behaved mob should be.

SEJANUS

Johnson's *Sejanus* concludes with a mob scene in which the protagonist, beheaded for his treasonable contriving against Tiberius, suffers desecration from the "rude multitude" who tear his body to pieces. Writing in the classical manner, Johnson presents this climax by reportage, but it is no less graphic for that. Lest one look upon Shakespeare as unique in characterizing the populace as both uncontrollable and changeable, it is important to sample Johnson's more malignant efforts on the same theme. Terentius is speaking:

> The eager multitude (who never yet
> Knew why to love or hate, but only pleas'd
> T' express their rage of power) no sooner heard
> The murmur of Sejanus in decline,
> But with that speed and heat of appetite,
> With which they greedily devour the way
> To some great sports, or a new theatre,
> They fill'd the Capitol, and Pompey's Cirque
> Where, like so many mastiffs biting stones,
> As if his statues now were sensitive
> Of their wild fury; first, they tear them down;
> Then fast'ning ropes, drag them along the streets,
> Crying in scorn, "This, this was that rich head
> Was crown'd with garlands, and with odours, this

That was in Rome so reverenced! Now
The furnace and the bellows shall to work,
The great Sejanus crack, and piece by piece
Drop in the founder's pit."

Lep.   O popular rage!

Ter. The whilst the senate at the temple of Concord
Make haste to meet again, and thronging cry,
"Let us condemn him, tread him down in water,
While he doth lie upon the bank; away!"
While some, more tardy, cry unto their bearers,
"He will be censur'd ere we come; run, knaves,"
And use that furious diligence, for fear
Their bondmen should inform against their slackness,
And bring their quaking flesh unto the hook.
The rout, they follow with confused voice,
Crying they're glad, say they could ne'er abide him;
Inquire what man he was, what kind of face,
What beard he had, what nose, what lips? protest
They ever did presage he'd come to this;
They never thought him wise, nor valiant; ask
After his garments, when he dies, what death;
And not a beast of all the herd demands
What was his crime, or who were his accusers,
Under what proof or testimony he fell.
There came, says one, a huge long-worded letter
From Capreae against him. Did there so?
O, they are satisfied; no more.

Lep.   Alas!
They follow Fortune, and hate men condemn'd,
Guilty or not.

Arr.   But had Sejanus thriv'd
In his design, and prosperously opprest
The old Tiberius; then, in that same minute,
These very rascals, that now rage like furies,
Would have proclaim'd Sejanus emperor.

Lep. But what hath follow'd?

Ter.   Sentence by the senate,
To lose his head; which was no sooner off,
But that and th' unfortunate trunk were seiz'd
By the rude multitude; who not content
With what the forward justice of the state
Officiously had done, with violent rage

Have rent it limb from limb. A thousand heads,
A thousand hands, ten thousand tongues and voices,
Employ'd at once in several acts of malice!
Old men not staid with age, virgins with shame,
Late wives with loss of husbands, mothers of children,
Losing all grief in joy of his sad fall,
Run quite transported with their cruelty!
These mounting at his head, these at his face,
These digging out his eyes, those with his brain
Sprinkling themselves, their houses and their friends;
Others are met, have ravish'd thence an arm,
And deal small pieces of the flesh for favours;
These with a thigh, this hath cut off his hands,
And this his feet; these fingers, and these toes;
That hath his liver, he his heart: there wants
Nothing but room for wrath, and place for hatred!
What cannot oft be done, is now o'erdone.
The whole, and all of what was great Sejanus
And, next to Caesar, did possess the world,
Now torn and scatter'd, as he needs no grave
Each little dust covers a little part:
So lies he nowhere, and yet often buried! [6]

Even had Jonson staged this scene instead of employing re-portage, he would not have achieved a much greater realiza-tion of fury and veering, senseless collectivity. Nor is this the end of it, for the mob seizes "for farther sacrifice" a son and young daughter of the dead Sejanus. At the play's close, moreover, as though the gamut of mutability had not been run, the populace is told by Apicata that others should have suffered its blind vengeance. "What says now my monster, the multitude?" cries Arruntius. Nuntius replies that their gall is gone and they weep for their mischief.

Arr.   I thank 'em, rogues.
Nun. Part are so stupid, or so flexible
    As they believe him innocent; all grieve:
    And some, whose hands yet reek with his warm blood,
    And grip the part which they did tear of him,
    Wish him collected and created new. [7]

[6] Act V, scene 10, ll. 310-383.   [7] *Ibid.,* ll. 433-438.

Besides exhibiting a more than Shakespearean abandon in depicting the populace, Jonson provides some very pertinent topical data. In the dedication of *Sejanus* to Lord Aubigny he writes that it is a play which, "if I well remember, in your lordship's sight, suffered no less violence from our people here than the subject of it did from the rage of the people of Rome." Whether wryly comic or really indignant, this statement means that dramatists of the time could make some identification of their fictional populace with the actual one of the public theaters.

On the score of topical matters, Jonson also manages to include in his play one Cremutius Cordus, "a writing fellow" whose practice it is

> To gather notes of the precedent times,
> And make them into Annals; a most tart
> And bitter spirit, I hear: who, under colour
> Of praising those, doth tax the present state,
> Censures the men, the actions, leaves no trick,
> No practice unexamin'd, parallels
> The times, the governments; a profest champion
> For the old liberty— [8]

A more pungent Elizabethan description of the tendency to confect history with topical savor could not be produced; the statement is even more pointed than similar examples which have been reviewed in the preceding chapter. Nor does the case end with this, for in the third act this same Cremutius Cordus is arrested for publication of his "Annals" and charged specifically with "comparing men and times." [9]

EDWARD IV

Among playwrights of Shakespeare's time the difficulty of presenting mass assemblage with democratic sympathy was obvious. There were, however, points of view within the framework of orthodoxy which could be assumed by drama-

[8] Act II, scene 2, ll. 167–174.   [9] Act III, scene 1, ll. 374 ff.

tists who favored the common people, and within these limits it was possible to assert a vigorous democratic spirit. An analysis of *Edward IV* will demonstrate what this means. The second scene of the play opens with Falconbridge and his rout moving in rebellion upon the city of London. In the midst of a typical contemporary mob scene and following cries of "Liberty, liberty, liberty, general liberty!" Falconbridge shouts arrogantly that his followers are not in rebellion like "Tyler, Cade, and Straw" for "mending measures or the price of corn" or to resist enclosure abuses, but are worthy champions of state policy bent on restoring the "true and ancient lawful right of the redoubted house of Lancaster." This august spell is quickly broken, however, by a leveling manifesto equal to that of Shakespeare's Cade.

> We will be Masters of the Mint ourselves,
> And set our own stamp on the golden coin.
> We'll shoe our neighing coursers with no worse
> Than the purest silver that is sold in Cheap.
> At Leadenhall, we'll sell pearls by the peck,
> As now the mealmen use to sell their meal.
> In Westminster, we'll keep a solemn court,
> And build it bigger to receive our men.
> Cry Falconbridge, my hearts, and liberty!

And this is followed by similar promises of equalitarian debauchery made in harangues by Chub, Spicing, and Smoke, who are Falconbridge's proletarian lieutenants. Thus far the play is indistinguishable from the Shakespearean norm.

In the next scene, however, it becomes clear who is to resist the rebellion. The opposing force will be no muster of aristocrats, as in Shakespeare's Cade scenes and in *Jack Straw,* but will be the common citizenry of London: "whole companies of Mercers, Grocers, Drapers, and the rest." In Act I, scene 4, of Part I, the Lord Mayor calls up the memory of Walworth, mayor in Richard's time, and his quelling of the Straw-Tyler rising. This is immediately succeeded by appearance of the sturdy commoners in the play, the apprentices of London, who in answer to the Lord Mayor's rallying cry declare that "by the ancient custom of our fathers, we'll soundly lay it on." From the rebel side they are taunted by Spicing, who tells them that "when matters come to proof, you'll scud as 'twere a company of sheep." The reply to this is full of resolution and pride in low estate and of contempt for the outlanders.

> Thou term'st it better that we keep our shops.
> 'Tis good indeed we should have such a care,
> But yet, for all our keeping now and then,
> Your pilf'ring fingers break into our locks,
> Until at Tyburn you acquit the fault.
> Go to: albeit by custom we are mild,
> As those that do profess civility,
> Yet, being mov'd, a nest of angry hornets
> Shall not be more offensive than we will.
> We'll fly about your ears and sting your hearts.

And the first apprentice adds, after a brief colloquy,

> Nay, scorn us not that we are prentices.
> The Chronicles of England can report
> What memorable actions we have done,
> To which this day's achievement shall be knit,
> To make the volume larger than it is.

After "a very fierce assault on all sides, in which the Apprentices do great service," Falconbridge enters and damns his own rabblement with the abuse traditionally vented upon Elizabethan inciters of mass disorder.

> Why this is to trust to these base rogues,
> This dirty scum of rascal peasantry,
> This heartless rout of base rascality.
> A plague upon you all, you cowardly rogues,
> You craven curs, you slimy muddy clowns,
> Whose courage but consists in multitude,
> Like sheep and neat that follow one another.

Compare Cade's cynicism directed at his own following in *2 Henry VI*. Further parallels between *Edward IV* and the

Cade episode appear in the ensuing scene with reiteration by Falconbridge of the leveling cry,

> The Mint is our's, Cheap, Lombard Street, our own;
> The meanest soldier wealthier than a king.

To which is added Spicing's Cade-like announcement that when the city is won he shall have "the knighting of all these rogues and rascals."

The rebellion is finally crushed by the commoners, who are led by none other than Mathew Shore, husband of Mistress Shore. Further to be noted and emphasized is the fact that, as Falconbridge and Spicing plan to do each other in and capitalize upon the reward of a thousand crowns offered for their heads, it is not a gentleman like Shakespeare's Iden who is the nemesis of the rebels; it is a humble miller.

Throughout the two parts of *Edward IV* the role of the commoners, from poor artisans to substantial burghers, is not merely the putting down of rebellion; they are shown as a sober and intelligent political force, the backbone of public policy within the commonwealth. In Act IV, scene 4, of Part I, the king's officers seek to collect funds for war against the French. The scene is the country and the king's men treat with a number of landholders by announcing first that the king scorns to tax and "mildly doth entreat" for contribution. Hobs, a plain tanner, listens attentively to the elaborate speech of Sir Humphrey Bowes and replies with homespun good sense:

So th'feck and meaning, whereby, as it were, of all your long purgation, Sir Humphrey, is no more, in some respect, but the King wants money, and would have some of his commonty.

The squirming then begins, as several of the landowners try to evade responsibility. The prodigality of one of them is decried by Lord Howard with:

> Here's a plain tanner can teach you how to thrive,
> Keep fewer dogs, and then ye may feed men:

Yet feed no idle men; 'tis needless charge:
You that on hounds and hunting-mates will spend,
No doubt but something to your King you'll lend.

As another landholder, Grudge, is rebuked by Hobs for his evasiveness, he strikes back.

Gep, goodman Tanner, are ye so round? Your prolicateness has brought your son to the gallows almost. You can be frank of another man's cost.

And the tanner observes with affecting anger and sentiment:

Th'art no honest man, to twit me with my son: he may outlive thee yet, for aught that he has done: my son's i'th' gaol: is he the first has been there? And thou wert a man, as th'art a beast, I would have thee by the ears.

As Hobs' turn comes, he offers "Twenty angels and a score of hides." "If that be too little," he says, "take twenty nobles more. While I have it, the king shall spend of my store." The upshot is that good offices of intercession are promised for Hobs' son and that Grudge is shamed into making twice the lowly tanner's contribution.

Through Part I and most of Part II there is, moreover, a major emphasis upon the prodigal goodness and charity to the poor of another commoner, Jane Shore the king's mistress. It is her play and her husband's who, in the torment of his dubious position, shows a resignation in favor of the common good which must have drawn tears from devout and sentimental citizens in the audience. In spite of the sentimentality, the cross of royal adultery carried by both Shore and his wife is handled with a psychological sureness which is well up to modern standards. And in contrast to the villification she receives in Shakespeare's *Richard III,* Jane Shore attains at Heywood's hands a virtual canonization. Her deeds of good to the unfortunate and her influence for the public welfare are such that the adulterous Edward's queen, armed with a knife for the disfigurement of her rival, draws it, *and making as though she meant to spoil* Jane Shore's *face, runs to her, and falling on her knees, embraces and kisses her, throwing away the knife.*[10]

In the last scene of Part II, the deaths of Shore and his wife are recounted in sentimental lines which are memorable for their recognition of a grateful, sound-hearted populace. King Richard has asked Catesby, "Where died Shore and his wife?" Catesby answers,

> Where Ayre was hang'd for giving her relief,
> There both of them, round circling his cold grave,
> And arm in arm, departed from this life.
> The people, from the love they bear to her
> And her kind husband, pitying his wrongs,
> For ever after mean to call the ditch
> Shore's Ditch, as in the memory of them.

APPIUS AND VIRGINIA

By contrivance of the corrupt Appius, the daughter of Virginius has been adjudged a bondwoman and threatened with dishonor; to save her from this fate Virginius has killed her. Doom begins to close upon Appius in the fourth act with a mutiny of soldiers who choose Virginius as their general after he has entered the camp,

> and at his heels a legion
> Of all estates, growths, ages and degrees.[11]

This is the massed populace which has unpeopled half of Rome to support the just cause of Virginius and is joined by mutineers from the army.

The avenging force enters Rome to find Appius deserted by his followers. The second scene of Act V discovers the evil Appius and Clodius, his plebeian lieutenant, "fettered and gyved," and here occurs an episode as strange for its time as the affair of the righteous populace in *Philaster*. Appius opens the scene by cursing the mob for causing his downfall.

---

[10] Stage direction, Part II, Act II, scene 2.   [11] Act IV, scene 2, ll. 73-74.

> The world is chang'd now. All damnation
> Seize on the Hydra-headed multitude
> That only gape for innovation!
> O who would trust a people?

None would, agrees Clodius, save one "rear'd on a popular suffrage" and whose station is built on *aves* and applause. "The same hands," continues Appius,

> That yesterday to hear me conscionate,
> And oratorize, rung shrill plaudits forth
> In sign of grace, now in contempt and scorn
> Hurry me to this place of darkness.

To which Clodius rejoins, "Curse on the inconstant rabble!" They then fall to quarreling over which of them is bearing up best under degradation, Appius insisting in surly fashion that it is Clodius who is weak because he is unequipped with aristocratic fortitude.

The point to be made is simple, but important. Here we have the traditional assault upon the populace as hydra-headed, gaping for innovation, and more mutable than water; it is the old refrain again, but in a singular context. The traditional caricature of the populace is drawn by a double-dealing patrician whose protests about the mutable multitude carry a ring of insincerity and self-justification. It is as though such a multitude had risen against Richard III, who, being undone, had declaimed in hollow rhetoric all the Shake-spearean charges against the mob.

As the play ends, however, there are some qualifications of this; perhaps Webster felt that he had carried matters too far. In any event, as Virginius enters the prison to confront the criminal pair, he commands,

> And from this deep dungeon
> Keep off that great concourse, whose violent hands
> Would ruin this stone building and drag hence
> This impious judge, piece-meal to tear his limbs
> Before the law convince [convict] him.[12]

[12] Act V, scene 2, ll. 43–46.

As Appius and Clodius are offered the honorable course of suicide, moreover, Appius the aristocrat takes it while Clodius the pleb begs for mercy, which brings from Icilius a rhetorical observation about the "difference 'twixt a noble strain and one bred from the rabble." [13] A political balance is at least restored, but the plain truth remains that Webster's populace has acted in justice and is denounced by malefactors whose falsity infects all of their platitudes upon mob inconstancy.

Philaster AND *The Loyal Subject*

Well-informed people often make the observation that a militant assemblage of commoners is never presented sympathetically by writers of Shakespeare's time. If this were true it would not lessen the importance of the problem for reasons which have already been examined. It happens, however, that the generalization is not true, and some irony attaches to the fact that Beaumont and Fletcher supply one of the clear exceptions. For it is this pair of dramatists whose politics Wingfield-Stratford characterized as "abject flunkeydom" in contrast to the "manly Toryism" of Shakespeare.[14]

In *Philaster,* which was written not long after *Coriolanus,* the massed citizenry, with clubs and bills, save Philaster from the death decreed for him by their king. The play opens with political overtones in the first scene when Dion asserts that "the multitude, that seldom know anything but their own opinions," have declared themselves for Philaster, and against the Spanish Prince, on the issue of marriage to the king's daughter, Arethusa. In the same scene the multitude is described as cheering Philaster's appearance by throwing up hats and arms and proceeding, "some to make bonfires, some to drink, all for his deliverance: which wise men say is the cause the King labors to bring in the power of a foreign

---

[13] *Ibid.,* ll. 171–172.
[14] *The History of British Civilization* (New York, Harcourt Brace and Company, 1930), p. 485.

nation to awe his own with." In the first scene, moreover, Philaster is condescendingly given permission to speak his mind in the royal presence. This he does with great courage in utterance of some plain truths about Pharamond the Spaniard, declaring that if the latter becomes king through marriage, "Look I be dead and rotten, and my name ashes." At which the king judges him too bold even under the license granted him to speak, and calls for physicians to examine his sanity. This is a strange episode for two dramatists who are reputed to favor Stuart absolutism with "flunkeydom." Later in the opening scene, Dion, an influential antagonist of the Spaniard, comforts Philaster by telling him that in the name of his father,

> We'll waken all the gods, and conjure up
> The rods of vengeance, the abused people,
> Who, like to raging torrents, shall swell high,
> And so begirt the dens of these male-dragons,
> That, through the strongest safety, they shall beg
> For mercy at your sword's point.[15]

That this theme of popular uprising is intended as central and decisive is borne out again in the first scene of Act III. In prosecution of Philaster's cause against Pharamond, Cleremont remarks,

> Philaster is too backward in't himself,
> The gentry do await it, and the people,
> Against their nature, are all bent for him,
> And like a field of standing corn, that's moved
> With a stiff gale, their heads bow all one way.[16]

In Act IV, moreover, Philaster wounds Arethusa because of false charges that she has been unfaithful to him, and a homespun "country fellow" stands up to him. At Philaster's scornful, "Pursue thy own affairs, it will be ill to multiply blood upon my head," the commoner retorts simply, "I know not your rhetoric, but I can lay it on if you touch the woman."

[15] Act I, scene 1, ll. 322–327.   [16] Act III, scene 1, ll. 19–23

And as an outcome of this episode, when Cleremont prays "that this action lose not Philaster the hearts of the people," the intelligence of the populace is promptly vindicated by Dion. The popular rebellion in Philaster's favor breaks out climactically in Act V, and it is inspired by no Jack Cade, or pair of seamy tribunes, or a rabble-rouser like Antony. It is the upright Dion instead who, as forces are mustered to rescue Pharamond from the aroused citizens, says to himself of the latter, "O brave followers! Mutiny, my fine dear company, mutiny!" And as the king shouts of the populace, "A thousand devils take 'em!" Dion in another aside mocks him with, "A thousand blessings on 'em!" Action begins. Of the citizenry, Dion now shouts,

Are your swords sharp?—Well, my dear countrymen what-ye-lacks, if you continue and fall not back upon the first broken shin, I'll have you chronicled and chronicled, and cut and chronicled, and all-to-be-praised and sung in sonnets, and bawled in new brave ballads, that all tongues shall troul you in *saecula saeculorum,* my kind can-carriers.[17]

Here is the anomaly of them all. It is the respectable Dion's wish that, for a change, the stormy populace be blessed rather than villified in literary annals. There could hardly be a more conscious dramatizing of the fact that Philaster is supposed somehow to make amends to the common citizenry for all the patronizing and falsification which has been its lot at the hands of playwrights. The passage would be surprising enough in any play of Shakespeare's age, but when it is made to follow a heavy emphasis, apparent from the beginning, of the citizens' part in sound politics, it is clearly startling. A strong topical note, moreover, is injected here. Dion's phrase "what-ye-lacks" means shopkeepers, so called from their cries to passers-by, and the phrase is echoed in the next scene as the leader of the citizens, an "old captain," shouts to them, "Forget your mother gibberish of 'what do you lack'

17 Act V, scene 3, ll. 129–137.

... and then cry Philaster, brave Philaster!" Tradesmen of London could not have been unmoved by this. With inflamed zeal the citizens threaten the Spanish prince, whom they have in custody; one of them in fact asks permission to geld him. Philaster appears at this tense moment, is hailed by the citizens, thanks them with emotion, and even calls them "gentlemen." The Spaniard, now freed, relinquishes all with

> I'll quit this land for ever. There is nothing,—
> Perpetual prisonment, cold, hunger, sickness
> Of all sorts, of all dangers, and all together,
> The worst company of the worst men, madness, age,
> To be as many creatures as a woman,
> And do as all they do, nay, to despair,—
> But I would rather make it a new nature,
> And live with all those, than endure one hour
> Amongst these wild dogs.[18]

And the "wild dogs" are congratulated, rewarded, and sent to their homes for honest celebration of the blow they have struck for good government. The play closes as the king abdicates in favor of Philaster, approves the latter's marriage to Arethusa, and referring to the popular uprising which has occurred, closes the play with a moral,

> Let princes learn
> By this to rule the passions of their blood:
> For what heaven wills can never be withstood.

Shades of James I!

The role of the populace in *Philaster* has been considered by Mrs. Mary Grace Muse Adkins in a recent article.[19] While she calls attention to the functional nature within the play of the popular uprising and is concerned with the unusual character of the populace in *Philaster*, Mrs. Adkins is nevertheless unconcerned specifically with the relationship of this to the mob theme in Jacobean drama. Her chief interest is in

[18] Act V, scene 4, ll. 110–118.

[19] "The Citizens in *Philaster*: Their Function and Significance," *St. in Ph.* XLIII (1946), 203–212.

the bearing of the play upon the current divine right concept;
she is rightfully insistent upon the emphasis made of divinity
which hedges the king, and she correctly notes the surprise
to be derived from the populace as a dramatic agent of justice,
even though the king is a usurper. Mrs. Adkins, however, is
extremely cautious: first, she writes that the citizens, "except
for the serious business of securing the kingdom, are made
objects of more or less kindly ridicule" ("ungrudging, but
realistic admiration" would perhaps be more accurate);
secondly, she feels that because the dramatists were writing,
not a play based upon English history, but one "romantic in
scene and story," they therefore did not intend to face the
political issue squarely; and thirdly, although Mrs. Adkins
declares that the play gives "evidence of the changing temper
of the English people," she suggests no relation of *Philaster*
to contemporary trends other than its appearance "at a time
when James himself temporarily relaxed his extreme claims."

The first of these assertions will have to be judged by readers from experience with the play itself and by application
of their own notions of what "kindly ridicule" is and what it
implies, especially after comparison with *Coriolanus*, where,
according to orthodox critics, kindly ridicule is also the dominant point of view. Mrs. Adkins' second assertion denies unconsciously the main contribution of her article, which is an
outspoken argument that the play did face the issue by em-
phasizing repetitively the political function of a massed
people. If, moreover, romantic setting is to be considered
evidence that the issues raised in Elizabethan literature are
not faced squarely, it is hard to imagine what we ought to
conclude about *The Merchant of Venice*, Spenser's episode
of the giant and the scales, or the mob scene in Sidney's
Arcadia. Had these been given an English historical setting,
would they have carried more ethical weight than they do?
In one sense, of course, the claim is valid; a setting too immediate, a state of affairs too realistically presented in Shake-

speare's day invited prompt action by the censor (witness the
Ill May Day scenes), and this was one of the good reasons
why dramatists dealt in the remote. Audiences knew this,
however, and were more prone than those of today to infer
contemporary meaning by "comparing men and times."

As for Mrs. Adkins' third point of view, that *Philaster*
bears relation to contemporary affairs only in that James I
had relaxed his demands for royal authority, there is a much
more specific set of historical events running from about
1604 onward, to which the play has an almost obvious application. In that year there were efforts by James to negotiate
a marriage between Prince Henry and Anna Maria, Infanta
of Spain. The king, who admired Spanish absolutism, sought
the international peace which such an alliance would have
fostered, together with a shoring-up of the monarchy at home
which freedom from external conflict would have effected.
Philip III, however, demanded certain concessions as the
price, among which were toleration for Catholics and education by the Spanish mother of any issue of the marriage.
Negotiations broke down for the time being, but were re-
opened in 1611 at the instance of the Spanish ambassador.
Anna Maria having been promised by that time to Louis
XIII of France, her younger sister was substituted as Prince
Henry's intended bride. And although the death of Prince
Henry in 1612 put a temporary end to negotiations, they
were later resumed, with Prince Charles as the prospective
bridegroom. This, of course, is not the whole story of the conciliation and solicitation of Spanish power by James, and it
is needless to describe the unpopularity of such a program
with a strongly Protestant and Puritan English public. Some
of the events just recounted occurred, of course, after the
writing of *Philaster,* but since the play continued to be staged,
the problem of audience response to its impingement upon
contemporary politics remains the same.

Application of this drawn-out state of affairs to *Philaster* is both immediate and compelling. A reading of the play or of the synopsis just given will reveal that the entire grievance of the populace is that the king wishes to marry his daughter to Pharamond the Spanish prince, and "labors to bring in the power of a foreign nation to awe his own with." The rising of the populace, that "fine dear company" of "what-ye-lacks," is the means whereby an infamous selling out of domestic liberty to foreign domination is accomplished. It may be recalled also that the king in the play is a doctrinaire expounder of absolutism, which makes the parallel complete. Those familiar with the tendency of Jacobean audiences to find in many plays a representation of contemporary events will recognize a topical issue here, even in the unlikely event that none was intended by the dramatists.

Whether or not the foregoing interpretation is correct, we still have in *Philaster* a play which runs completely counter to the trend of previous drama, including that of Shakespeare, which was to anathematize mass assemblage for political action. Here the populace in arms is the guardian both of political liberty and national security. And to anyone who is prone to find in the absolutist behavior of Coriolanus a generalized commentary upon the flaunting of popular support by James I, the comparison between *Philaster* and Shakespeare's play, written only a short time before, is doubly interesting. For in Shakespeare the populace, particularly through its tribunes, is damned with a tragic thoroughness equal to if not more pronounced than that bestowed upon the aristocratic protagonist.

How a play so opposed in concept to *Coriolanus* as *Philaster* escaped the censor is hard to fathom. The editions of 1620 and 1622 specify public acting of the play at the Globe, and Chambers mentions two court performances in the winter of 1612–1613. It should be observed that Fleay, noting the extensive variations present in the first quarto of I.1 and V.4, suspected that these were alterations made for

the performances of 1612–1613. An examination of these
variants, however, shows that they do not differ markedly
from other editions so far as the political content, relevant
here, is concerned. The first edition is as forthright on this
theme as the subsequent printings. The only suggestion which
can be offered to explain the lack of censorship is that public
feeling, both popular and aristocratic, was so aroused by
conciliation of Spain that a play which heralds a militant
populace as the ultimate bulwark of independence and constitutional liberty became, strangely enough, acceptable.

The charge of "abject flunkeydom" made by Wingfield-
Stratford against Beaumont and Fletcher is based mainly
upon *The Loyal Subject,* and it is undeniable that the political significance of this play is reactionary. In Acts IV and V
there is a headlong rebellion of common soldiers who rescue
Archas, their general, from infamous torture and disgrace.
But Archas, who has the combined submissiveness of Job
and Griselda, greets his deliverers with this constitutional
gem:

> I charge ye, as ye are men, my men, my lovers,
> As ye are honest faithful men, fair soldiers,
> Let down your anger! Is not this our sovereign?
> The head of mercy and of law? who dares, then,
> But rebels scorning law, appear thus violent?
> Is this a place for swords, for threatening fires?
> The reverence of this house dares any touch,
> But with obedient knees and pious duties?
> Are we not all his subjects, all sworn to him?
> Has not he power to punish our offences,
> And do we not daily fall into 'em? Assure yourselves
> I did offend, and highly, grievously;
> This good sweet prince I offended, my life forfeited,
> Which yet his mercy and his old love met with,
> And only let me feel his light rod this way:
> Ye are to thank him for your general,
> Pray for his life and fortune, sweat your bloods for him.[20]

[20] Act IV, scene 7, ll. 44–60.

The rebellion persists, however, until at the close of the play Archas succeeds in controlling it and asserts in even stronger terms his quixotic belief in divine right. It would be agreeable to say with one critic that *The Loyal Subject* is one of the plays which exhibit "persistent assumption of good-will and right-headedness" in the popular masses.[21] The good will is there, but if any attention is paid to choral pronouncement in the play, the moral is that good will implemented by popular rebellion is the ultimate in wrong-headedness. Moral ambivalence, of course, may be present in that an audience would naturally experience sympathy for the rebels, but it must be remembered that the sternest kind of moralizing is that which forcibly reminds an audience of its irrational sympathy with evil conduct. In this sense Miss Ellis-Fermor's appraisal of the good will and right-headedness of the mob in *The Loyal Subject* is accurate, for she asserts that with Shakespeare's mobs "there is a sinister implication behind the voluble excitement" which gives "veracity and soundness" to the total picture. It is presumed that this veracity means an agreement between the unfavorable Shakespearean portrait of the mob and the repudiation of it in his plays, which does contrast with the romantic picture of the rebels, followed discordantly by their "realistic" rejection in *The Loyal Subject*. In any case, the latter play must be viewed as quite opposite to *Philaster* so far as democratic implications are concerned. In *Philaster* the uprising of "what-ye-lacks" is blessed from the beginning, and there is no dissonance between its benevolent character and the ultimate favorable judgment passed upon it. It thus remains an anomaly both within the general frame of Elizabethan and Jacobean drama and the specific one of Beaumont and Fletcher.

The peculiar nature of *Philaster* is again accentuated by comparison of it with *Sir Thomas Wyatt*, by Dekker and Webster, a play which also dramatizes popular rebellion for

[21] U. M. Ellis-Fermor, *The Jacobean Drama* (London, Methuen and Company, 1936), pp. 222–223.

the preservation of England against Spanish domination.
Here is to be found another instance of the equivocal and
ambivalent treatment of mass rising when the rebellion serves
laudable ends, a treatment basically similar to that of *Appius
and Virginia;* Wyatt himself is allowed to suffer a martyr's
fate, with assertion of noble motives and willing sacrifice,
but upon the populace which supported him is placed an onus
of excess and instability which is analogous to the checks
which Webster puts upon the populace in *Appius and Virginia,* after it has served its worthy purpose. A qualification
is thus made which is the opposite of the clear praise bestowed
upon the citizens in *Philaster.*

Of these contemporary portraits of democracy in action,
three may be called Shakespearean in attitude. And to these
three, which are *Jack Straw,* Spenser's episode, and *Sejanus,*
may be added the uprising of commoners in Book II of Sidney's *Arcadia,* description of which would be both lengthy
and unnecessary. In the resulting "Shakespearean" group of
two representative plays and two representative narrative
episodes, the satire upon mob leveling and mob fickleness
squares with the attitude explicit in the Cade scenes, *Julius
Caesar,* and *Coriolanus.* Of the items which parallel Shakespeare, *Jack Straw* contains a minor hint, similar to the one
in *Coriolanus,* that the commons have a grievance, a hint
which is quickly passed over in both plays. It is noteworthy,
however, that in the four pieces which have been likened to
Shakespeare's work there is no employment of the "rank
scented" theme which is so characteristically his. Only in occasional plays, such as Lyly's *Alexander and Campaspe,*
where there is a reference to foul breath of the Athenian
populace,[22] and Marston's *Malcontent,* where there is an
allusion to "stinkards," [23] does a suggestion of crowd stench
occur. No one will question that the notion of a smelly popu-

[22] Act III, scene 1, l. 25.   [23] Act V, scene 1, l. 39.

lace occurs sporadically in the patrician attitudes of most, if not all, historical periods; the issue here is the conception which occurs in all the "mob plays" of a single dramatist and is expanded into thematic repetition in his most significant play of that group. While in *Jack Straw, Sejanus,* and the two episodes of Spenser and Sidney there is every other detraction of the mob which was characteristic of Shakespeare, there is still a notable absence of this ruling motif.

The remainder of the representative plays, which comprise a kind of control group for qualitative analysis of Shakespeare, show major deviations from his standard practice, and all these deviations are favorable to the populace as a political force. *Sir Thomas More* projects the usual wrong-headedness of the citizens, but ends upon a strong note of their tractability and contriteness, which is notably missing in Shakespeare's recognized work. If Shakespeare wrote the Ill May Day scenes of this play, he made a sentimental exception to his general rule. Heywood's *Edward IV* not only exhibits a populace attractively loyal and generous but deviates greatly from the Shakespearean standard by placing the massed citizenry in a position of political responsibility, for London is saved from rebellion in this play by common Londoners of the kind who had seen and were to see themselves lampooned by other dramatists as political cowards and zanies. *Edward IV* presents this remarkably changed point of view not only in plot but also in plentiful choral moralizing. Heywood's play, moreover, grants to substantial bourgeois commoners, typified by Mistress Shore and her husband, the most honorable of parts in the maintenance of public welfare. It should not be forgotten that in a romantic age a socially inferior but rising class will seek romantic expression of itself, and that the Elizabethan commoner found in dramatists such as Heywood and Dekker relief from the satirical and "realistic" humiliation which came his way from other sources.

When we come to *Appius and Virginia,* in which Heywood

also may have had a hand,[24] another dramatic phenomenon appears, that of actual popular uprising which realizes a laudable and intelligent purpose. Although it must be recognized that the populace is partially repudiated at the end of this play, there are still redeeming themes in the sound part it plays and in the evident insincerity with which the evil victims of popular wrath are made to mouth all of the current platitudes anent mob disorder.

Philaster, however, is the genuine oddity. It is from dramatists who in other respects were of deserved reactionary repute that a play appears which contrasts politically in every important way with its contemporary, Coriolanus. The populace revolts, is favored with choral praise, and saves the legendary kingdom from a state of affairs only too parallel to the state of England. And in contrast with Edward IV or Appius and Virginia there is neither a lawless populace balanced against the loyal one nor limited disapproval of the praiseworthy rebels once they have accomplished their purpose. There is no hedging and no apology. It may be remarked, of course, that the citizens revolt in Philaster against a king who is a usurper, and this will suggest, perhaps, that the play is therefore not the anomaly it appears to be. Against this qualification a reminder should be entered, however, that the conspirators in Julius Caesar are also, in a manner of speaking, usurpers and that if Shakespeare had followed the pattern of Philaster the Roman mob of his play would have been explicitly approved for its action. Philaster remains, in a way, hardly less startling than the Henry IV plays would have been if the usurper Bolingbroke had been limited in power by an aroused populace of which choral approval had been declaimed. The only fundamental difference is that Shakespeare would have been forced to alter publicly known history in order to have achieved such an episode.

There is again the temptation to admit that dramatists

[24] Chambers, The Elizabethan Stage, III, 508–509.

may be controlled by the sources they use rather than by political bias. It can be asserted, for example, that Shakespeare's three plays were unlike certain others of the "control group" in that they did not come from sources in which the populace served commendable ends. And it might be added that *Philaster* could exhibit freedom in its treatment of the citizenry because there was no controlling source from which a political theme was derived. The rejoinder to this qualification is one which has been hinted at before, but needs to be reasserted here. When an Elizabethan dramatist or a modern novelist chooses a story from history, from fiction, or from the alternatives suggested by his imagination, his social point of view is likely to be antecedent to his selection of plot and is likely to control that choice. Even if the inherited story runs somewhat counter to his social point of view, there are endless opportunities for selective emphasis, and the dramatic emphasis bestowed by Shakespeare upon his source material scarcely indicates the social tendencies shown by *Edward IV* or *Philaster;* it often runs counter, in fact, even to the temporizing ambivalence of *Appius and Virginia* or *Sir Thomas Wyatt.*

CHAPTER VI

Literature and Social Disintegration

MOST INTERPRETERS of the Cade scenes, *Julius Caesar,* and *Coriolanus* have sought to remove Shakespeare from the stigma of political negation or pessimism; traditional criticism has done its best to find his view of the populace either humane and wholesome or else judicious because it followed convention. That it was conventional cannot be questioned, except for the reminder that some other dramatists were more generous to the common people. But that Shakespeare presented a pessimistic estimate of *demos,* however conventional it may have been, does not seem to be the conclusion many have wished to accept. Nor has their reluctance diminished when emphasis is placed, as it has been here, not upon Shakespeare's private opinions or motives, but upon the calculated reaction of audiences to the plays.

This apologetic view is part of a much larger problem in literary interpretation and can best be met by encountering the greater issue. The activities of social satirists and analysts who have used the literary medium invite from time to time the charge that what they write is decadent, disruptive, cynical, and one-sided. It has become usual in recent years to refer to such literature as sick. Literature is sick when it goes on all fours with the human animal and sick when it tries to emphasize the rational; when it descends to propaganda and when it attempts to be tentative; when it cultivates a large audience and when it is written for the few; when it has no ethical values and when it is controlled by tight moral systems. It is sick, moreover, when it dwells upon social collapse, and sick when it avoids facing social collapse squarely. What can the poor author do to become normal, poised, and part of a going concern? The advice sometimes given him if he is a modern is that he try to remember Shakespeare, and the conception of Shakespeare implied by this is mysterious, almost as mysterious as the conception one still encounters of the Elizabethan period as integrated, extroverted, optimistic, and sound. Elizabethan England, of course, was none of these things to any remarkable degree, nor was Shakespeare. One is tempted to say that his great talent was dedicated to synthesis of good and evil into balanced normality, but it is often hard to say it. It is true that Shakespeare honestly faced the consequences of mental, emotional, and social illness; this he did, perhaps to an exaggerated degree, but so do many moderns who are accused of the ripest decadence. The point here will be that in exploiting disintegration, individual and social, an author fulfills one of the usual functions of literature, whether he compensates for the disintegration or not.

Failure to recognize this historically normal tendency leads to constant recurrence of an old critical practice, that of excoriating poets, playwrights, and others for magnifying the evils of a society and ignoring its virtues. Thus, Puritan critics of Elizabethan drama emphasized the arrogance, ambition, cruelty, incest, rebellion, and butchery which were "the matter of tragedies," [1] and attacked chronicle plays for historical falsehood.[2] In our own time Mr. Bernard DeVoto has written with scorn of literary men because they dwelt upon "the decadent civilization, the blindness and depravity and disgusting stench of an evil nation," while scientists were quietly inaugurating Reclamation and a new era in medicine.[3]

[1] I. G., *A Refutation of the Apology for Actors* (1615), ed. by R. H. Perkinson, pp. 55–56 (Scholar's Facsimiles and Reprints, 1941).

[2] *Ibid.*, p. 42.

[3] *The Literary Fallacy* (Boston: Little, Brown and Company, 1944). The ensuing statement of Mr. DeVoto's case is taken from Chapters II, IV, V, and VI.

Plainly, to this cast of critical mind a demonstration that Shakespeare reverted constantly to the stresses and cleavages of a tottering society should not add to his credit, nor should the later Jacobean dramatists be left unremarked upon for ignoring the vision of Bacon or the discoveries of William Harvey.

A conventional reply to such castigation is to remind the over-serious that literature and life are different things and, with Professor Stoll, to explain that the characters of Restoration drama, for example, are not reflections of mass corruption, but are instead fictional effervescences of a society on the whole serious and religious.[4] From this conventional standpoint the Wastelanders of our own era, far from deserving Mr. DeVoto's rebuke for libeling society, should be accepted as a manifestation of literature rather than of life, and the mobs of Elizabethan drama viewed as variations on a constant literary theme rather than as indications of any actual social condition.

The trouble with this standard explanation or defense of social distortion in literature is that it is both obvious and inconclusive. In it the literature-life problem is forced into factitious issues: whether Othello's behavior is that of a real Moor among real Venetians; whether the Canterbury pilgrims are the kind of people one would have known in medieval England; whether O'Neill's characters are authentic "cases" representing prevalent forms of neurotic behavior. The answer to all such queries is, of course, one of breezy denial, which sets nobody right except the naïve, who, it is true, are often tempted into literal identification of fiction with reality.

Faced on one hand with the blaming of writers for social falsification and on the other with a bland excuse that such falsification stems from the very nature of literature, we are driven to ask what a poet, a novelist, or a playwright is sup-

---

[4] "Literature and Life," in *Shakespeare Studies* (1927), Chapter II.

posed to do in order to qualify as an accurate historian of his age or, in any event, to escape classification as a distorting agent of the life about him. Traditional skepticism is scarcely relevant here. Trained historians, whether amateur or professional, are not prone to conclude that affirmative or cohesive elements were absent in Elizabethan society when they are faced with evidence that Elizabethan drama dwelt continually upon disruptive social forces. They thus hardly need to be reminded of the strictures Mr. DeVoto thought necessary in interpreting the social scene drawn by writers of our own age. Nor do most historians need the warning of Mr. Stoll; they are not likely, for example, to conclude from the Cade scenes, *Julius Caesar,* or *Coriolanus* that Shakespeare's England was unusually threatened with popular revolt or disaffection.

Conventional reminders that appearance belies reality do not require, however, that historians abandon literature as social data. It is not necessary to observe of the world of science that knowledge begins rather than ends with a simple premise that things are not what they seem, but it is apparently necessary to draw upon this platitude in order to avoid standard forms of doubt which impede the study of literature as a reflection of society.

For circumvention of these skeptical positions but two assumptions are needed. First, it is not modern literature which has begun the distortion of life by preoccupation with social and individual disintegration. Mr. DeVoto surely knows that literature did so in the age of Shakespeare and that there was little new about the practice then. Secondly, literature of neither the present nor the past offers us norms of day-to-day experience; it provides instead, even when realistic, the undercurrents of triumph and frustration, of virtue and vice, of integration and disintegration which are prevalent as a kind of mythology among the people written to or written about. Mr. Stoll would agree to this, but would conclude from it either that literature is unreliable social data or that it is restricted to data which reveal "universals" and literary conventions rather than local or contemporary conditions.[5] The first of our two assumptions implies a simple course of inference. Before we express surprise that the literature of any period has dwelt upon human failings and a crumbling social structure, we should ask whether there is something in the nature of fiction to which such allegedly evil leanings are accountable. Greek drama, of course, can be cited as enveloping human shortcomings and excesses which when given a modern setting such as one finds in the work of O'Neill and Jeffers will be viewed by many as impious and morbid. Biblical narrative and folk ballads contain similar elements. If an actual society were to be constructed from the *Canterbury Tales,* a great majority of its members would range from pleasant materialists such as the Monk, the Prioress, and the Wife of Bath to moral nihilists such as the Friar, the Pardoner, and the Summoner. It should be remembered, moreover, that Chaucer's pilgrims are a very pleasing group when compared with the corrupt characters of *Piers Plowman.* Even so, should one be solemn enough to insist upon estimating English medieval society with the Canterbury Pilgrims as norms, the result would suggest little of promise, little of the serious reformative quality which Miss Helen White traces from medieval to seventeenth-century times in her outline of the Piers Plowman tradition.[6]

Shall it be inferred, then, after the manner of Mr. DeVoto in dealing with modern writers, that Chaucer was frivolous and decadent or that he had a jaundiced preoccupation with social corruption? It would be simpler and more to the point to conclude something quite different: first, that no writer is likely, or perhaps even able, to give us a well-proportioned

[5] "Literature and Life Once More," in *From Shakespeare to Joyce* (New York, Doubleday, Doran and Company, 1944), pp. 50–51.

[6] *Social Criticism in Popular Religious Literature of the Sixteenth Century* (New York, The Macmillan Company, 1944).

view of both the affirmative and the negative elements found in his society; and secondly, that many writers, perhaps most writers, are primarily effective when they take the negative view. In support of this claim, which is not a prescription, but an attempt at historical description, there may be cited in addition to authors already mentioned, Cervantes, Rabelais, most Elizabethan and Jacobean dramatists, Donne, Milton, Bunyan, the Restoration dramatists, Pope, Swift, Smollett, Byron, a good many Victorians, and all the moderns denounced by Mr. DeVoto. And such a list would be fragmentary.

If reasons are now sought for the predominance in fiction of negative, disintegrative, or venal elements of experience, there are several from which selection may be made. First, it is obviously difficult, although by no means impossible, for writers of fiction to present affirmation in such a way that suitable emotional responses will be evoked. For what reason is Spenser more interesting when showing vice opposed to virtue than when showing affirmative virtue opposed to vice? How is it that most people prefer *Othello* to *The Tempest?* Why, to call up trite comparisons, is *Paradise Lost* so much better than *Paradise Regained* or Wordsworth so much more difficult to present to students than is Byron? How does one explain that Arnold's *Dover Beach* is perhaps the best known of his poems? Why is it that when an author seeks to show goodness and rationality upon a social rather than upon an individual scale, he so often comes forth in artificial guise like that of *The Republic,* the *Utopia,* or *Lost Horizon?* What has impelled Aldous Huxley, in his more recent role of frank moralizing and social prescription, to accompany the strongly affirmative side of *After Many a Summer Dies the Swan* or *Time Must Have a Stop* with a quantitative overbalance of the earlier Huxley, the Huxley of *Point Counter Point?* Put plainly, one's answer is that the "wholesome," the "representative," and the "sound" will verge perilously toward uplift except in limited treatment by the most intelligent and tentative craftsman. A simple reason for this is that we are so called upon to show affirmative qualities in our routine lives that we seek in novels, plays, and poems an expression or a channeling of our impulses of negation. Perhaps this places a great deal of literature on a cathartic level with the soldier's gripe, but such a disposition is serious only to those who judge by means of connotative name-calling. To draw a parallel between literature and the commoner forms of negation is surely not a rationalization of literary insouciance, for intelligent negation can reach exceptional levels of penetration and sympathy; a little reflection will suggest that it is one of the chief solacing activities of collective man, a great leveler, and a prime astringent. It is not, however, the mere narcotic which such appreciation suggests, for it is well to remember that reform begins with negation if it is to begin at all.

If this amounts to a predicament in which writers and their readers find themselves, then let the predicament be expressed by Swift, who sensed it only too clearly.

For the materials of panegyric, being very few in number, have been long since exhausted. For, as health is but one thing, and has always been the same, whereas diseases are by thousands, beside new and daily additions; so all the virtues that have been ever in mankind, are to be counted upon a few fingers; but his follies and vices are innumerable, and time adds hourly to the heap. Now the utmost a poor poet can do, is to get by heart a list of the cardinal virtues, and deal them with his utmost liberality to his hero or his patron: He may ring the changes as far as it will go, and vary his phrase till he has talked round; but the reader quickly finds it is all pork, with a little variety of sauce.[7]

So much for the first premise. We may recall that the second suggested assumption was that literature, even when realistic, presents a mythology or lore of good and evil rather than normative behavior. It is not original to say that Hamlet, Manfred, and Hans Castorp "typify" their respective

[7] From the Preface to *A Tale of a Tub*.

ages only in the special sense of embodying, each of them, a current intuition of the alien individual beset with environmental hostility and disintegration. It is unnecessary to hunt for real Jack Cades or Charley Andersons beyond recognizing in both of them a group apprehension of the common man's befuddlement, in the one case a hostile apprehension, and in the other a sympathetic one. Shakespeare's or Daniel's Wars of the Roses are no more real than the Civil War of *The Birth of a Nation* or *Gone with the Wind;* yet all these in their turn present mythologies of civil dissension which nicely characterize the periods for which they were written. It is true that such examples are drawn from romantic literature, but the same limitations apply to highly disciplined and unsensational modern realists. The world of Proust is one of ironic introspection and total recall, as far removed from the stream of average life as is the world of *An American Tragedy,* but must we deny the validity of either as evidence of contemporary preoccupation with the significant? Literature, whether romantic or realistic, deals in crisis; and conceptions of thought, feeling, or behavior in crisis are materials of which significant mythology is made. Even such subdued realists as Elizabeth Bowen, who avoid contrived crises, confirm this view by their subtlety and understatement; important to them is a significant crisis-undercurrent, the mythology of an otherwise insignificant event or situation. If these things are true, the one remaining point to be granted is that the mythologies of an age are among the most revealing and real elements of it.

But what has the foregoing discussion to do with interpretation of mob scenes in Elizabethan drama? It may be repeated that Elizabethan mob scenes present disintegrative social forces and that these forces were not what they literally appear to have been in the actual scenes. This book throughout is an attempt at historical interpretation which will avoid traditional skepticism concerning the social realism of such literature.[8] In this final chapter we have considered a few simple arguments against the rejection of literature as social data merely because it runs counter to normal affirmative qualities present in any age (Mr. DeVoto's view) or because it presents "universals" instead of the routine behavior patterns sought for in more literal investigation (Mr. Stoll's view). Our general problem has been to investigate a body of literature in which stress has been laid upon social cleavage and collapse. Because the first of two assumptions has controlled interpretation, a prevalent view of this has been avoided. Many literary historians have sought to explain away a theme regarded, particularly in Shakespeare's case, as unworthy—unworthy because it involved social attitudes which were disintegrative; here a contrary course has been followed by assuming that when viewed historically much of the best literature has expressed and channeled the social elements of negation which the critics mentioned have found alarming.

Finally, the controlling effect of our second assumption has been to steer interpretation toward social undercurrents rather than toward surface actuality; specifically, Elizabethan mob scenes have been ascribed to an irritation in the air, a lore built upon fear of the social leveling which, according to conservatives, was implicit in the rising nonconformist tide. The social reality reflected by these scenes is hence the reality, not of literal conditions, but of an influential mythology. In our own day it is asserted that American liberalism is dominated by extremist forces, and the mythology of this hardly denies its reality as a social factor. Certain modern publicists make this charge; many of them believe it and many act upon it. Similarly, official Elizabethan opinion sought to link all nonconformity with the Anabaptist uprising, the Peasants' Revolt, the Cade rebellion, and with outbreaks of

---

[8] There has been no assertion, however, that social historians can use the fiction of a period without corroborative data from other sources.

the Roman populace. Many Elizabethans doubtless believed this, and many acted upon it. The mob scenes of Elizabethan drama partly reflect this mythology, but nevertheless exhibit a very real temper of Elizabethan society.

Index

Actors, satire upon, 73
Adkins, Mary G. M., on role of populace in *Philaster,* 172 ff.
Admonition to the People of England . . . , *An* (Cooper), 111, 132
Ainsworth, Henry, 128
Albions England, 130
Alexander and Campaspe (Lyly), 178
Allen, J. W., 93
Anabaptists, attempt to associate, with nonconformists, 106 ff., 132, 141; militancy in Germany: refusal to separate religious from social reform, 106; linked with Puritans, 119, 121, 129 f.; Ormerod's charges against, 129; association of, with peasant uprising and Hacket's revolt, 138; Spenser's arraignment, 156; *see also* Communism, "Anabaptistical"
Anglicanism, propaganda against opponents of, 107
Annales (Stow), 145
Anna Maria, Infanta of Spain, 174
Antibrownistus Puritanomastix, 142
Antony and Cleopatra, allusion to smelly populace, 69, 70
Apologie for John Wickliffe (James), 141
Apology for Actors (Heywood), 146
Appius and Virginia (Webster), 72, 181; populace, 167-69; uprising which realizes laudable and intelligent purpose, 180
Arcadia (Sidney), 173, 178
Aristocracy, not devoted to bathing and oral hygiene, 71; sins and shortcomings of, 86
Art, whether reflection of or influence upon social evolution, 6; primary purpose of, 8
Arthington, Henry, 102, 117, 119
Artistic forms, evolution of, 5
Assemblage, *see* Popular assemblage
Aubigny, Lord, 162
Auden, W. H., on art and social evolution, 6 ff.
Audience, calculation of temper of, 27, 30; orientation by "tables turned" device, 40, 42, 51-53, 68, 69; equipped with governing idea at beginning of play, 46-49; satire upon, 73; response to plays, 92, 93; political unrest apparent to, 98; preconceptions, associations, and prejudices, 99; as it witnessed Cade scenes, *Julius Caesar* or *Coriolanus,* 148; prone to find contemporary meaning in plays, 174, 175; moral ambivalence of, 177; relief of in Heywood and Dekker from satirical humiliation, 179

Bacon, Francis, 184
Ball, John, 135, 141
Bancroft, Richard, on the populace, 103; compared with Hooker, 105; on nonconformists, 109 ff., 113, 134, 156; confused Cade's rising with Peasants' Revolt, 135
Barker, Christopher, 113, 118
Barlow, William, 130, 137
Baronial instability, condemnation of, in history plays, 79
Barrow, Henry, 116
Beard, Thomas, 146
Beaumont, Francis, and John Fletcher, treatment of populace, 167, 169-78